The Agony of Asar

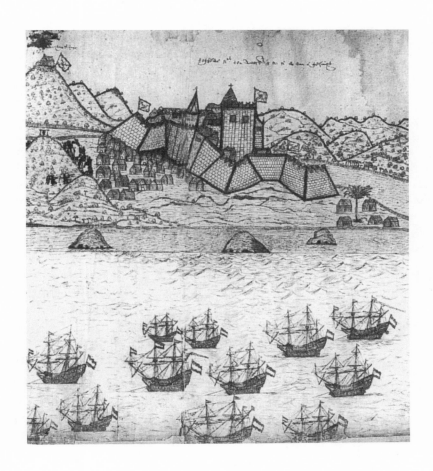

STAATKUNDIG-GODGELEERD ONDERZOEKSCHRIFT
OVER
De Slaverny, als niet ſtrydig tegen de Chriſtelyke Vryheid,
WELK,
ONDER HET GEHENGEN VAN DEN ALGENOEGZAMEN GOD,
En de Voorzittinge van den Hoog-Eerwaarden en Wyd-Beroemden Heere
JOAN VAN DEN HONERT, T. H. SOON,
Doctor der Heylige Godgeleerdheid; Profeſſor in dezelve Wetenſchap, en in de
Kerkelyke Geſchiedeniſſen, in de Hollandſche Univerſiteit; en Predikant
in de Gemeente des HEEREN te LEIDEN,
Aan eene opentlyke en gematigde beproeving onderwerpt
JACOBUS ELISA JOANNES CAPITEIN, een MOOR uyt AFRICA
SCHRYVER EN VERDEDIGER.
Uyt het Latyn vertaalt door HIERONYMUS DE WILHEM.
De vierde Druk.

TE LEYDEN, {BY PHILIPPUS BONK,}
TE AMSTELDAM, {BY GERRIT DE GROOT.} 1742.

Cover page to Capitein's dissertation,
translated by H. de Wilhem (fourth printing, 1742)

THE AGONY OF ASAR

A Thesis on Slavery
by the Former Slave,
Jacobus Elisa Johannes Capitein,
1717–1747

Translated with commentary
by Grant Parker

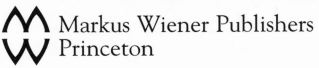 Markus Wiener Publishers
Princeton

For information write to:
Markus Wiener Publishers
231 Nassau Street, Princeton, NJ 08542, U.S.A.

Library of Congress Cataloging-in-Publication Data
Capitein, J. E. J. (Jacobus Elisa Johannes). 1717–1747.
    [Dissertatio politico-theologica de servitute libertati Christianæ
non contraria. English]
    The agony of Asar: a thesis on slavery by the former slave,
Jacobus Elisa Johannes Capitein, 1717–1747 / Jacobus Elisa
Johannes "Capitein"; translated by Grant Parker;
edited and with an introduction by Grant Parker.
    Originally presented as the author's thesis—
Leyden University, 1742.
    Includes bibliographical references and index.
    ISBN 1-55876-125-x (hc)
    ISBN 1-55876-126-8 (pb)
    1. Slavery and the church—Reformed Church.   2. Reformed
Church—Doctrines.   I. Parker, Grant.   II. Title
HT913.C36   1996
261.8'34567—dc20   95-48329   CIP

First published in Jamaica 2001 by
Ian Randle Publishers
11 Cunningham Avenue, Box 686, Kingston 6

ISBN 976-637-036-2 paper
    A catalogue record of this book is available from the National Library
of Jamaica.

The hardcover edition of this book includes a facsimile
of the original Latin text of Capitein's thesis.

Contents

Foreword

Jacobus Elisa Johannes Capitein, the former slave who defended slavery by claiming it does not contradict Christianity, has had a mixed reputation ever since he died in 1747 at the age of thirty. But for much of the time since then he has been more known about than known, and for that reason the humble task of this book is to present accessibly the treatise that has earned him his reputation. I hope it will nourish the interest of students of the history of slavery, and indeed of anyone interested in its diverse aspects. Furthermore, questions of church and state, of race and ethnicity, and of the history of scholarship are addressed throughout these pages. The special historical significance of the treatise is twofold: it presents us with an 18th-century African intellectual of extraordinary learning, and it implies that the Netherlands of his time harbored more antislavery sentiment than has usually been supposed (see section IV.2).

The aim of my translation has been to provide a version that can be easily understood, sentence by sentence. As a result I have not been able to do full justice to Capitein's rhetorical style, which is elaborate and intricately crafted, in keeping with its classical model, Cicero. It was after all originally composed for oral delivery. Indeed, the baroque qualities of the text have sometimes set the goals of accuracy and comprehensibility at odds with each other: I hope the end result reflects a reasonable compromise. My own comments in the introduction and endnotes are merely offered as ways into the text; the real task of analyzing Capitein's treatise itself rests squarely on the reader's shoulders. The tripartite appendix also offers additional material for the study of Capitein and his world, partly by outlining the lives of other figures with whom he can be compared.

It was only after completing a first draft of the translation that I became aware of David N. A. Kpobi's version appended to his monograph on Capitein, *Mission in Chains* (1993). But I decided to go ahead nonetheless, for three reasons: firstly, Kpobi's translation was made from a Dutch translation rather than the original Latin (p. 185), and, though contemporary, this Dutch version has its own eccentricities; secondly, Kpobi's work was written for a more specific readership than the one I have in mind, and this affects the commentary he gives (see appendix 3 below); and, thirdly, the book is not widely available outside of the Netherlands. The very recent appearance of Henri van der Zee's Dutch biography of Capitein, 's *Heeren Slaaf* (2000), suggests that he continues to attract interest.

For a small book this has brought me many debts of gratitude, which I am pleased to acknowledge.

My heartfelt thanks are due, in the first instance, to Robert Shell, who several years ago invited me to undertake this project with him as a joint venture. I deeply regret that he later withdrew, so that we were not able to work together on it; so I am all the more grateful for his blessing on my subsequent efforts.

Having been trained in Classical Studies rather than African or slave history, I was at first hesitant to take on a task such as this: someone in my position may well have been advised to stick to his day job. But my motivations were two-fold. Firstly, I believe that the later appropriations of Greco-Roman antiquity provide a rich area of inquiry in their own right, quite apart from enriching the study of the ancient texts themselves. In presenting this work as part of what might be called the classical tradition I wish to draw as much attention to its own social context as to the nature of its continuities with antiquity. E. J. Hobsbawm has aptly attuned us to the "invention of tradition," and I believe Capitein's uses of the past should be seen in this light. The second reason is more personal: being both a scholar of ancient literatures and the descendant of a slave society (in fact of Dutch slavery too, but at the Cape of Good Hope instead), I have had the chance to reflect in my own ways on the issues presented by Capitein's life and writing. It seems to me, sadly, that the heritage of slavery is far from being deeply appreciated in South Africa, even as the official end of apartheid ushers in a reconfiguration of social memory. I hope this connection has lent more engagement than bias to my account of Capitein, but again it is for readers to decide if this is so in practice.

At various stages Peter Brown, David Brion Davis, David Gordon, Anthony Grafton, Emily Mackil, Daniel Rothenberg, and Robert Shell were kind enough to read through drafts of the manuscript, making suggestions of substance and detail. H. D. Cameron and Gregson Davis graciously discussed parts of the translation with me, and I am deeply thankful for the trouble they took. I am also grateful to the Department of Historical Studies at the University of Natal, Durban, for the opportunity to present parts of my manuscript to their lively research seminar; I merely regret that a tight schedule has made it impossible for me to integrate more of their suggestions and insights. In the latter stages Richard Parker and Shauna Shaw assisted with the proof-reading, helping me to sharpen my phrasing at countless points. Needless to say, I alone am responsible for the errors and oversights that remain.

For encouragement and advice of various kinds I am grateful to all of the above, and also to Mamadou Diouf, Elizabeth Elbourne, Ian Farlam, Kweku Garbrah, Simon Gikandi, Robert Harms, Bernhard Kytzler, Paul E. Lovejoy, Christopher Stray, and Robert L. Tignor. Conversations and correspondence with them have guided and assisted me more than they may realize. Ruth Scodel helped me with Capitein's use of Hebrew.

Special thanks are due to Jim Mackil, who scanned most of the illustrations and helpfully advised on presentation; and to James B. Summit, who originally produced the maps. Emily

Mackil also provided much-needed help with computing matters, and generally helped keep things in perspective. I also thank Janice Chen and Melissa Holcombe, research assistants of Robert Shell years ago, who helped with the original compilation of materials.

Susan Lorand has been a perceptive and tactful editor: her readiness to go the extra mile at the crucial final stages has been much appreciated. I thank Cheryl Mirkin for her innovativeness in the design process. Last but not least, without Markus Wiener this project would have foundered in the years between its conception and realization. I owe much to his initiative, practical help, and good humor.

On a different note, I owe sincere thanks to the Michigan Society of Fellows and to the Department of Classical Studies, both of the University of Michigan, for conferring on me a post-doctoral fellowship without which this project would not have come into being. At Ann Arbor I've had both the precious time to pursue the project and a supportive, stimulating environment in which to do so: a young scholar could not hope for better. The Harlan Hatcher Graduate Library and Clements Library have been a joy to use.

For permission to reproduce illustrations and documents, I thank the Amsterdam University Library (one portrait of Capitein); the H. Henry Meeter Center, Calvin College, Grand Rapids, Michigan (portrait of Calvin); the Clements Library, University of Michigan (four early maps); and not least the Leiden University Library (for the original Latin treatise and the remaining illustrations).

To all the above, and to any I may have omitted by mistake, my warmest thanks. Finally, I should like to dedicate this book to my parents, Mavis and Richard Parker, with gratitude and affection.

Grant Parker
Ann Arbor, Michigan, October 2000

THE AGONY OF ASAR:

An introduction to the life and work of Capitein

Amsterdam personified, receiving the bounty of the continents (Africa in the center). From Olfert Dapper, Historische beschryving der stadt Amsterdam *(Amsterdam, 1663). Leiden University Library*

An introduction to the life
and work of Capitein

> The educated Negro, slave of the spontaneous and cosmic Negro
> myth, feels at a given stage that his race no longer understands him.
> Or that he no longer understands it.
> Then he congratulates himself on this, and enlarging the differ-
> ence, the incomprehension, the disharmony, he finds in them the
> meaning of his real humanity. Or more rarely he wants to belong to
> his people.
>
> —FRANTZ FANON*

I t may come as a surprise to contemporary readers that
an 18th-century scholar should have argued for the
compatibility of slavery and the Christian faith, and
should in effect have defended the moral legitimacy
of such bondage. The surprise would be heightened if it is
added that the person arguing this case had himself once
been a slave.

These are precisely the supposed anomalies that are central to any encounter with the "political-theological" treatise translated here. Its title, "Is slavery compatible with
Christian freedom or not?", translates the original Latin,
*Dissertatio politico-theologica, qua disquiritur, Num libertati
Christianae servitus adversetur, nec ne?* It was published in
the university city of Leiden in 1742. Jacobus Elisa Johannes Capitein (1717–1747), its author, was born on the west

---

* from "Black Skin, White Masks," trans. C. L. Markmann (New York: Grove Press,
1967), p. 16.

coast of Africa, where he was enslaved as a child. He eventually attained his freedom and studied in the Netherlands before returning to Africa as a missionary, where he died at an early age.

What factors could have motivated such a person to defend slavery? Is it even feasible to try to reconstruct these factors? In one of only two English-language books to be devoted to Capitein, he has not surprisingly been dismissed as an "Uncle Tom," to reflect his apparent co-optation to the interests of his masters;[1] the task of these comments will be to reassess that analysis of his treatise and his life. By way of introduction to the translation of the treatise itself, the following pages are offered with two main purposes in mind: to show the nature of Capitein's own contribution to debates about bondage, and to demonstrate in what ways Capitein was a product of his times. These are in a certain sense contradictory purposes, but they are necessary to a mode of intellectual history that is alert to both human agency and social context, one that tries, in fact, to keep the two in a productive tension.[2] A somewhat different but certainly comparable contradiction may be summed up as follows. In order to understand Capitein, we need to understand what slavery meant in the world that he inhabited; yet equally, Capitein's story and treatise themselves inform us about that slave-holding world. It is here that slavery's intellectual history sits squarely, though uneasily, with its social and economic history.

Many questions and issues arise from the treatise. Most

obvious are those that relate the author to his work. The relevance of these cannot be denied, especially when the overtly autobiographical aspect of the treatise is compared and contrasted with other slave narratives, a genre of writing that has attracted much scholarly interest in recent times. But these are far from the only ones. Capitein's scholarly project calls for an assessment on its own terms: how is authority constructed and deployed in the treatise? As the endnotes added to this edition attest, the work bristles with learning. But it is not enough merely to note the many references and allusions made, whether to classical literature, to the Bible, or to medieval and early modern scholarship. Ultimately, we should like to know in broader terms what was at stake when a particular scholarly authority was invoked. Is it valid to compare different instances of slavery in a transhistorical manner, as Capitein does? What, in particular, is the sense of slavery that Capitein abstracts and compares over such a broad sweep of western culture? To be sure, the range of the work is tremendously ambitious. It is no perversity to see Capitein's use of his sources as problematic when many of them contain difficulties of interpretation within themselves. The Greco-Roman texts offer no single, abstract theory of slavery, however widespread are the references to bondage that may be found within their pages; and the same can be said for the Hebrew and Christian scriptures. This fact sits uneasily with Capitein's frequent citations and references. A more sympathetic analysis would follow the contours of his selectivity, and be attentive to the choice of the many 16th- and 17th-century scholars that he mentions and quotes. Finally, the issue of race, in its full range of cultural and somatic aspects, requires consideration. Explicitly, it is present in the treatise in an ethnology linked with the Bible; implicitly, its many aspects pervaded the life of someone who spent his life alternately as an African-born former slave in the Netherlands and as a Dutch-trained minister of religion (*predikant*) in Ghana.

These, then, are some of the issues that demand our attention in the pages that follow. They are offered in an attempt to grasp various aspects of Capitein's historical context, and to use Capitein himself to understand the world that he inhabited. Constantly we need to bear in mind both the theory and the practice of slavery. Capitein participated, on one hand, in an intellectual (philosophical and theological) debate about the moral legitimacy of the institution; on the other, bondage was part of the concrete experience of his life, as it was for some eleven or twelve million people transported across the Atlantic by various European maritime powers between the early 15th and the late 19th centuries.[3] It is reasonable to expect that theory and practice should have related to one another in this, but it is also challenging to understand the complexities of that relationship.

I. A life: servitude and aftermath

1. An orphan in the Netherlands

Jacobus Elisa Johannes Capitein, as he was later to be known, was born in 1717 in the immediate hinterland of the Guinea coast, an area that is part of modern Ghana (see map 2).[4] Orphaned at the age of seven or eight, he was sold into slavery at St. Andrew's River, and later he spent some time at the coastal trading posts of Elmina and Shama.[5] His master, the sea-captain Arnold Steenhart, gave or perhaps sold him to his friend, Jacob van Goch, who had by that time served the Dutch West India Company (WIC) for fifteen years.

When Van Goch left Elmina for the Netherlands on April 14, 1728, he took Capitein with him, "so that I might practice some trade that was not demeaning and thereby earn a living," as Capitein was later to write. Their destination was Middelburg in the Dutch state of Zeeland. Here Capitein attained his freedom. It was freedom by default, since slavery had been effectively outlawed when the Dutch Republic came into existence as a result of the international treaty of 1648.[6]

Still in the company of Van Goch, he moved after a short time to the Hague, the home-town of Van Goch, where he remained for several years, learning the Dutch language and also the art of painting. Here, too, the largesse of the Reformed minister Johann Philipp Manger (1693–1741) allowed Capitein to join catechism classes in preparation for baptism into the church. Contacts made during these classes, through fellow pupils who were the sons of eminent burghers, led directly to the furthering of his formal education. The theologian Henrik Velse (1683–1744), prompted by his young son, suggested that Capitein receive further opportunities for study, on the condition that he later devote his life to Christian missionary activity in West Africa. Capitein consented, although his account of this episode seems curiously tentative. His patron Van Goch added both his approval and his practical support. The subvention of other burghers made it possible for Capitein to attend the Hague Latin School. One of these patrons was F. C. Roscam, an aristocratic woman who acted as both a teacher of the ancient classical languages of Hebrew, Greek, and Latin, and as a benefactor.[7] Another was the influential Leiden jurist Peter Cunaeus, who funded part of Capitein's university studies through the generosity of the Hallett Fund.[8] On July 8, 1735, after four years in this school, Capitein was baptized at the Kloosterkerk by Manger, his original catechism teacher.

It was at this point that he took on his first three names: Jacobus Elisa Johannes, after his patron Jacobus van Goch, after Van Goch's sister Elizabeth, "who has been like a second mother to me," and after Van Goch's niece Anna (Johanna) Mulder, who was also the wife of Van Goch's cousin, Pieter Nesker. The three acted as witnesses at his

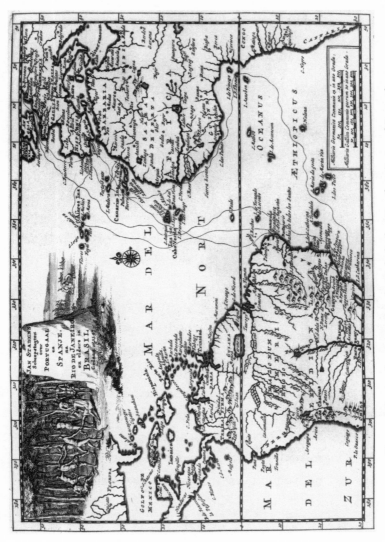

Pieter van der Aa, Sea-routes from the Netherlands to Brazil via Spain and Portugal, from Cartes des itineraires (1728). Clements Library, University of Michigan

baptism. He had been given the name Capitein on his arrival in the Netherlands. Of his original name we cannot be sure: nineteenth-century sources report his name as Asar, but the source of this information is now lost. It is possible that the name is a mistaken distortion of the name *Afer*, the Latin for "African."[9]

Capitein's six-and-a-half years of schooling in the Hague ended in 1737 with a public lecture that was later published as the treatise "On the calling of the heathen" (i.e. on the need to call them from their error of unbelief; in Latin *de vocatione ethnicorum*). Although the work is no longer extant, Capitein's summary of it at the beginning of his longer treatise, and indeed its title, make it clear that Christian mission was at the forefront of his agenda, at least in the scholarly-religious sphere of his life.

This schooling qualified Capitein for further education at the University of Leiden, where, as university records attest, he registered on June 22, 1737, to study theology. He again received the hospitality of burghers, living during his five years at Leiden in three different households. Financial support for his university studies also came from Van Goch, from the Hague Latin School, and from the university itself. It is possible that the level of his funding, some of which was contingent on satisfactory progress, went beyond the norm.[10]

The treatise which is translated here was delivered as a lecture on March 10, 1742, and represents the culmination of his studies at Leiden. It marked his attainment of one of the predoctoral degrees, the Master's or more probably the Licentiate.[11] Such occasions were formal to the point of ritual: all participants were duly attired in their academic finery. A candidate would present his lecture before the faculty's full assembled professoriate, and thereafter answer their questions. Unlike the procedure in most contemporary Protestant universities, the lecture would represent the candidate's own work, rather than that of his professor.[12]

Capitein's ordination into the Dutch Reformed Church by its governing body, the Classis of Amsterdam, followed on May 7 of the same year. This could happen only when he had been appointed by the WIC, for it was the Company that paid missionaries as its own employees.[13] Together these developments opened the way for Capitein to return to Guinea, and this he did without delay in early July 1742. In the intervening time his Latin treatise, "Is slavery compatible with Christian freedom or not?", had been published in Leiden. Capitein dedicated the publication to Peter Cunaeus and his other sponsors, as he says in the introduction. So popular was his work to become that it was translated into Dutch in a matter of months, with four new editions appearing within the year.

2. Unhappy returns: Elmina, 1742–1747

The source for most of the above information is Capitein himself, while the records of the University of Leiden add some details about his studies there. Certainly the autobiographical passage that precedes the treatise itself deserves close attention (see his "Preface to the reader" below). For his subsequent life, a number of letters survive from his correspondence with the WIC and the Classis of Amsterdam. Together they give the impression that the remaining five years of his life were beset by practical difficulties, and disagreements with both the WIC and the Classis.

Arriving back in Elmina on October 8, 1742, Capitein assumed the spiritual leadership of both the WIC employees, based at its headquarters in the Castle, and also of the school attached to the headquarters.[14] Within his sphere of ministry there were 107 staff of the WIC at Elmina, out of a total of 241 on the Guinea coast. Initially Capitein made a good impression on the WIC's director-general in charge of the west coast region, Jacob de Petersen, who wrote a favorable report about him immediately after his service of induction on October 21, 1742. The text of the sermon that Capitein delivered at that service, II Corinthians 4:6, is significant for its implied presentation of himself as the "light shining out of darkness." Clearly the dual purpose of his mission was to uphold the morale of the Dutch employees and to convert Africans to Christianity.[15]

On his return to Elmina, Capitein was in many senses a different person from the one who had been taken as a slave to the Netherlands fifteen years earlier. Indeed, for this man of African descent, now leading a supposedly European life, the question of acculturation and reassimila-

Fishermen outside Fort Elmina. From Jean Barbot, A Description of the Coasts of North and South Guinea (London, 1732; original French edition Paris, 1688). Leiden University Library

tion soon became an acute one in this familiar but unfamiliar setting of Elmina. His letters suggest that his attempts to reintegrate himself into African society did not meet with the greatest success—not surprisingly, given that in the preceding years the Dutch slaving activity at Elmina had intensified. Capitein himself wrote to the WIC, at a time when he was eliciting its approval for his plan to marry a young African woman, in order "to win the affection and trust of the blacks here at Elmina." In this letter, dated February 17, 1743, Capitein hints ominously that the state of the Christian church at Elmina was worse than he had expected. His intention to marry an African woman, he says, was to show goodwill toward the local population and thus further his task of conversion.[16]

Capitein's plan to marry became the first of a series of differences that he was to have with his superiors in Amsterdam. The woman, whose name is not recorded, could not legitimately marry him without first being baptized; and it was not acceptable that Capitein, as husband-to-be, be the one to teach her the catechism, and the woman's parents were unwilling for her to travel to the Netherlands to receive instruction there.[17] The Company's solution to this problem was a high-handed one: it sent a Dutch woman from the Hague to marry Capitein, apparently without giving him any forewarning. There are many puzzles about the woman, Antonia Ginderdros, and the circumstances of her journey. For example, had she known Capitein before? What was her background in the

View of Fort Elmina from the land

Aerial view of
Elmina from the sea

Netherlands?[18] In any event, the marriage took place on October 3, 1745.

By this time, however, it is clear that Capitein's relations with both the Classis and the WIC had deteriorated. Three letters from him to the WIC requesting practical assistance went unanswered, and its eventual answer to his fourth still exhibited an attitude of intransigence. On the other hand, the Classis wrote to express its displeasure with him, in part for his failure to report directly to it.[19] This letter, dated January 10, 1745, also reveals that the Classis had doctrinal differences with Capitein.[20] He had translated the Lord's Prayer, the Twelve Articles of Faith, and the Ten Commandments into Fante, a local dialect of the Akan language, which is a member of the Niger-Congo family. Aspects of the translation were considered unacceptable by the Classis, and it claimed that Capitein had circumvented its authority by dealing directly with publishers at Leiden rather than working through its agency to obtain or ratify the translations. Some reservations about Capitein's translation of these religious texts were also shared by the publisher, Hieronymus de Wilhem, who took the remarkable step of expressing them in his own preface to the text: see Appendix 1 below. These disagreements give the impression that Capitein's original policy of evangelizing the Africans through the teaching of children was beset with enormous problems of a practical and even a theological nature.

Capitein died on February 1, 1747. There is no indication of the cause or the circumstances surrounding his death. It is clear, however, that by this time he was at loggerheads with both the WIC and the Classis. In a letter of May 23, 1746 to the Company, he had spoken openly of his personal unhappiness,[21] and he was already heavily in debt. While we know that a surgeon and a wine-merchant were among his creditors, we do not know the circumstances or any of the details of these debts.[22] Two months after his death, director-general De Petersen wrote in a letter to Amsterdam that Capitein's "craving for trade ... had dampened his zeal for religion."[23] Again, we might well ask what kind of trade Capitein had been engaged in, but the available sources do not clarify the issue.[24] The location of Capitein's grave in Elmina is not known.[25]

3. Potentially parallel lives: Equiano and Capitein

However skeletal the above sketch may be, it does invite comparison with the life of a well-known slave of the later 18th century, who also, once freed, wrote an account of his earlier years. Olaudah Equiano (1745–1797) was kidnapped at the age of 11, together with his sister, in the east of modern Nigeria.[26] Eventually sold to a British owner and renamed Gustavus Vassa, he arrived in Britain and fought in the Seven Years' War (1756–63). Rather than receiving his expected freedom at its conclusion, however, he was sent to the Caribbean, still in bondage. Here he was to work for another three years, initially ferrying passengers from one island to another and later trading in his own right. In the process he earned enough money to buy his own freedom and he then returned to London in 1766. Eight years later he converted to Christianity. His memoirs, which were published in 1788 as the *Interesting Narrative of the Life of Olaudah Equiano*, were widely read in Europe and by 1791 versions had appeared in Britain, the United States, the Netherlands, Germany, France, and Russia. In 1792 he married an Englishwoman, Susan Cullen, who died three years later after bearing two children. Within the abolitionist movement of the late 18th century, Equiano's memoirs were read as an indictment of the slave system, and its closing pages contain an overt denunciation of slavery. He himself, as a public lecturer in his final years, became an outspoken activist for abolition.

Equiano left a fuller story of his life, and we know more about his time as a slave than we do of Capitein's: his work tells his own story, partly in the interests of exposing the horrors of slavery. Equiano spent a longer time in servitude, and, unlike Capitein's, a substantial part of his servitude was as an adult. There is no indication that Equiano's married life was an unhappy one nor that his spell in commerce involved trading in slaves. A point of similarity between the two men is their baptism into Christianity and, subsequently, a pride in professing the faith. In fact Capitein's "autobiography" is no memoir, but merely an apologia with which to introduce his treatise. Equiano, on the other hand, was by no means a scholar, engrossed in the learned theological and philosophical debates of contemporary academia. Even if he was able to read and write English, his education was not focused on the Greek and Latin classics. The education that he did receive was not intended to make him a missionary, and in fact he spent his final thirty years in Britain rather than in Africa or the Americas.

Self-evidently, the comparison can only take us so far. For one thing, Equiano was a slave to British owners, not Dutch. Even more importantly, by his own lifetime the abolitionist movement had gained much momentum, and it had its champions in the British statesman and evangelical Christian, William Wilberforce (1759–1833), and others. By this time large parts of the church explicitly denounced slavery. But nonetheless these few points are worth noting in an attempt to characterize Capitein's life. Some further points of comparison and contrast will be considered under section III below.

II. The West Indies Company and the Dutch slave trade

1. The birth and slow demise of a seaborne empire

Let us consider in broader historical terms the role of the Netherlands in the slave trade, in order to understand better a person who lived his entire life within its sphere. Dutch participation in the Atlantic slave trade is an enormous topic in its own right: suffice it for our purposes to make a few important, if well-known points.[27]

As has been noted above, slavery had effectively become illegal in the Netherlands since its unification in 1648, which caused Capitein to become free upon reaching the Netherlands from the West African coast. This phenomenon has been termed implicit metropolitan manumission.[28] In the second half of the 17th century Dutch slave-traders made various attempts to establish markets at the main ports of Amsterdam and Middelburg, but in each case their efforts were thwarted by the local authorities. In effect, double standards prevailed, for Dutch merchants were heavily involved in the slave trade at a considerable geographical distance from the Low Countries. These, it might be said, were the double standards well known to colonial situations; in fact, the same phenomenon has been powerfully illustrated in the case of France in the Ancien Régime.[29] In 1713 a decree of the Dutch East India Company (VOC) determined that any slave who set foot in the Netherlands automatically became free upon arrival. From as early as the 1650s this had been the practice in the city of Amsterdam. In some parts of the Netherlands, owners who tried to keep slaves were prosecuted.[30]

Ongoing European contact with the West African coast (Guinea) dates back to expeditions initiated by Prince Henry of Portugal between 1421 and 1445. In 1481 the

Portuguese set up a permanent presence there by building a castle at São Jorge da Mina (Saint George of the mine) at Elmina in modern Ghana. From here they hoped to gain access to the hinterland's gold supplies: both the centuries-old trans-Saharan gold trade from the western Sudan, and the river-washings of Ghana itself. The goal of penetrating the interior was, however, not reached until the European colonization of Africa in the 19th century: for some considerable time, the inland of West Africa was to prove largely inaccessible to European colonists. Yet from the mid-15th century, and especially in the 16th, the trans-Atlantic slave trade was to reach tremendous proportions. Portuguese and Spanish traders used their monopoly in long-distance seafaring to traffic in slaves between the west coast of Africa and the newly discovered Americas. By the end of the 15th century the Portuguese had established "factories" (*feitorias*) or trading posts down the West African coast as far as present-day Angola, and in the early 16th their factories were extended to east Africa and the sea-route to south Asia.

In sketching the transition from the Portuguese to the Dutch trade monopoly on the Gold Coast, it is important to mention also a transition from the import to the export of slaves. In the 16th century, slaves were one commodity among many imported by the Portuguese in exchange for the all-important export, gold. Other goods imported by the Portuguese into the Gold Coast included cloth and beads. The slaves were brought to the Gold Coast from

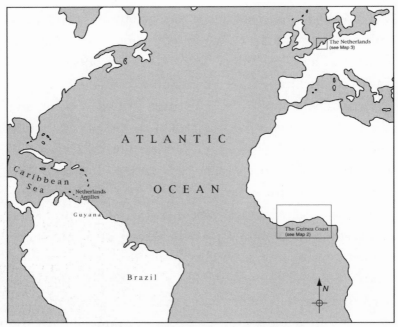

Map 1. *The Atlantic world in the early 18th century*

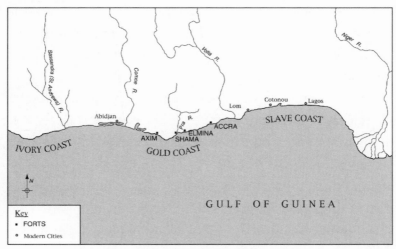

Map 2. *The Guinea Coast*

Map 3. The Netherlands

Benin and the Niger delta. They were needed mostly as mine-laborers and porters. At the coast gold-dust was exchanged for much bulkier goods, and these needed to be carried back into the interior, even when tsetse fly and forest conditions limited the use of cattle as beasts of burden.[31] The Gold Coast became a net importer of slaves by the early 17th century, but it was not until the final three decades of the century that the sale of slaves took on great economic importance, outstripping gold in Dutch commercial interests here.

Commerce in persons reached a peak in the first half of the 18th century. In the first decade of the century, an average of some 2,500 slaves were sold every year, a figure which continued growing to around 4,700 per year in the 1710s, 7,300 in the 1720s, 8,600 in the 1730s and climaxed at 9,100 in the 1740s. From the 1750s the trade declined by about 25 percent and then continued to fall, despite a brief recovery in the 1780s. A major factor in the rise in slave sales in the first part of the 18th century was the conflict between groups of Akan people of the Gold Coast and its hinterland. Warfare in the region substantially increased the supply of slaves, at the same time as the demand for them in the Americas, not least in the Dutch Caribbean, was high. The victors in the conflict were the Asante, who proceeded to build a considerable network of trade routes centered on their inland base of Kumase, and in fact Dutch slavers depended very heavily on the Asante in this period and subsequently.[32]

In his assessment of the struggle between the Portuguese and the Dutch seaborne empires between 1598 and 1663, C. R. Boxer has vividly shown that there were three simultaneous areas of conflict: that over the Indian Ocean spice trade, that over the slave trade of West Africa, and that over the sugar trade of Brazil. Broadly speaking, these three areas produced a victory for the Dutch in Asia, a draw in West Africa, and a victory for the Portuguese in Brazil. In the case of Africa, the conclusion of peace in 1663 brought the Dutch only mixed results because the Portuguese retained Angola, Benguela, São Tomé and Príncipe, though the Dutch had entrenched their position in West Africa north of the equator.[33]

Columbus' expedition to the Americas in the 1490s marked the beginning of a period in which Spain and Portugal forged trading contacts with the Americas, with each country setting up their own trading empire. The Iberian presence in the New World brought with it a high demand for slave labor throughout the 16th century. This supply was fulfilled by the contract system (*asiento*), by which the Spanish crown sold exclusive trading rights to an association of merchants. Some Dutch traders also took part in this system. The breakdown in the Iberian *asiento* system in the 1640s coincided with the Dutch ascendancy, and a shift in the bulk of trans-Atlantic slaving from Brazil to the Caribbean. At the same time, a shift from tobacco to sugar took place in agriculture, notably in the Antilles islands. The Dutch system, which focused on plantations, was shared in the same period but in different regions with British and French traders. It was Britain and France who would later gain the upper hand over the Netherlands. This Second Atlantic system, as it has been called, has usually been characterized as the birth of modern capitalism, for it was more geared to the maximizing of profits. It has been seen as a market-driven economy, subject more directly to the iron law of supply and demand, with the state intervening much less than the Spanish crown had done. The population of the Caribbean contained a much higher percentage of slaves than did the south Atlantic, and this boosted the intensity of agricultural production in the plantations.[34] If these Caribbean plantations, more than anything else, intensified the demand for labor, it was the West African coast that supplied it.

The fortified settlement of Elmina, forcibly taken by the Dutch from the Portuguese in 1637, was to retain its status as the headquarters of regional commerce into and even beyond the 17th century, a period which saw the ascendancy of the Dutch over the Iberian overseas trade.[35] The takeover of the fort marked the end of the Portuguese presence on the Gold Coast, and pointed forward to the zenith of Dutch overseas trade, roughly from 1647 to 1672.[36] Despite the Portuguese monopoly in the late 16th century, individual Dutch merchants had already been trading on the west coast of Africa since the 1590s. The Netherlands' first trading post had been established at Mori or Mouri, also known as Fort Nassau, in present-day Ghana, in 1612, and by 1621 Dutch activity on this coast had eclipsed that of the Portuguese.[37] An attempt by the Dutch to seize Elmina in 1625 had failed, but the takeover thirteen years later did provide them with a steady base from which to conduct their trade.

The Dutch West India Company (the *Westindische Compagnie*, or WIC), which was founded by charter in 1621, within a few decades made the Low Countries a major player in the Atlantic slave trade, although the Netherlands was a late arrival in a system that had already existed since the 1440s.[38] The WIC was formed on the model of the older East India Company (the *Verenigde Oostindische Compagnie*, or VOC, chartered in 1602), with the difference that from the start the WIC was expected to take an aggressive role toward the existing Iberian empires of the Atlantic. Significantly, its interests were protected by law: it had an official monopoly in all Dutch trade and navigation with the Americas and West Africa for more than a century. Within the Dutch colonies the WIC was legally entitled to make war and peace with the indigenous peoples, to maintain naval and military forces, and to carry out judicial and administrative roles. In the course of the 17th century the Dutch took over the Portuguese-held slaving areas on the Atlantic coast of Africa, and via their port of Curaçao they became a major supplier of slaves to the Spanish colonies. For some short periods of the 17th century the Netherlands came to dominate the entire Atlantic slave trade.

It comes as something of a surprise, then, to note that

WIC warehouses in Middelburg, Zeeland

"the Dutch entry into the Atlantic slave trade was more by accident than by design."[39] The WIC's participation in the slave trade was by no means obvious from the start. At its foundation in 1621, a vigorous debate took place between the Company's shareholders to decide the issue. After all, gold, rather than slaves, was intended to be the main focus of the WIC's activities; and in practice, Dutch traders on the African coast were at this point trafficking mainly in that precious metal. Different views prevailed as to the legitimacy of such participation in the slave trade, and the opinions of theologians were solicited. No consensus was reached till the late 1620s, and the WIC avoided commerce in slaves for the first decade of its existence. Theological legitimization for the trade in slaves in this period was not a rare thing, particularly in contexts where the "curse of Ham" (or Canaan) was invoked (see section III.1 below); on the other hand, since the 1590s the port cities of Middelburg and Amsterdam had shown their unwillingness to permit the establishment of slave markets. The intellectual issues of Dutch anti-slavery sentiment will be discussed below under section IV.2; for the present, it is sufficient to recognize that the Dutch did not become involved in the Atlantic slave trade until a relatively late stage, and then with a tangible degree of hesitation that can be linked to domestic debates about its legitimacy.

In economic terms, the slave trade should be seen in the broader context of long-distance commerce. By this time the Netherlands had become the first country other than

WIC headquarters in Middelburg, Zeeland

Spain and Portugal to build a substantial colonial empire. To an even greater extent than the Iberian empires, the Dutch trading empire aimed at commercial predominance rather than territorial hegemony for its own sake. Though the Dutch did come to control substantial areas of Java and Sri Lanka, such aggrandizement was always incidental to the economic power linked with them. In the case of the Cape of Good Hope, its settlement was undertaken reluctantly and with a view to strategic interests, rather than with a specific drive for territorial control. As J. L. Price has put it, "the Dutch did not acquire colonial territories for their own sake but only in the service of profit: ideally they would have preferred to limit their overheads by acquiring as little land as possible."[40]

The scene had changed radically by the 1730s, when pressure from free traders had reached new heights. By the end of the decade the Dutch monopoly was a thing of the past, having been eclipsed by British and French interests. Now the only two regions in which the WIC still dominated the slave trade were Guiana in South America and the Gold Coast (modern Ghana) in West Africa. Within three decades, the changed situation in which free traders predominated boosted the Dutch share in the slave trade once again, so that the 1760s saw another peak.[41] In 1734 the Company's monopoly of activities on the Gold Coast came to an end. The fourth Anglo-Dutch war of 1780–84 left the once-mighty Dutch navy in a much weakened state, and brought with it substantial territorial and trade losses in both the East and the West Indies.[42] As a seaborne empire, the Netherlands would never recover the ground that it lost to the British and French.

The Dutch role in the slave trade pales in significance when compared with that of the other maritime powers.[43] Dutch ships transported nearly 555,000 slaves from the African continent, and landed around 460,000 of them in the Americas.[44] Britain, Portugal, and France together accounted for some 8.6 million, or 90% of the total, with Portugal alone transporting about 35%. Unlike the Portuguese, the Dutch participated actively for a relatively short period, from around 1630 to 1795, during which time their share amounted to 7.5% of the total. At its peak, around 1760 to 1773, that may have reached 10%. For brief periods, such as from 1636 to 1648 when they supplied slaves to northern Brazil, they did predominate in the entire slaving system. Most of the slaves were taken to the Dutch Caribbean, especially Surinam, which received around 162,000 in the 18th century; Spanish America received 64,000 in the 17th century and 77,500 in the 18th.

Harder to evaluate is the general effect that the slave trade had on Dutch society in the 17th and 18th centuries. Certainly it is difficult to imagine the "embarrassment of riches" that the Dutch Golden Age was to become in the 17th century without the immense income generated by the overseas commerce in general, though of course the slave trade was only one part of that commerce.[45] And certainly, the vast network of the seaborne empire made the city of Amsterdam a particularly cosmopolitan place, a fact noted by a succession of overseas visitors to the Netherlands.[46]

But, lest we overestimate the effects of the slave trade on the Netherlands itself, two notes of caution should be sounded. Firstly, trade activity brought direct benefits to the port cities of Middelburg and Amsterdam, but not necessarily to the rest of the United Provinces of the Netherlands, and certainly not to the lesser-developed agricultural regions of the interior. Secondly, according to recent calculations, the profit margin of Dutch slave-trading did not exceed a modest 5%.[47] Slaving itself was thus not to prove a particularly lucrative business for the Dutch, all in all.

2. White man's burden: Christian mission

Both the VOC and the WIC employed missionaries in their colonies; the need for them was manifold. Firstly, the spiritual needs of Dutch workers abroad required looking after, and had a direct bearing on their morale and productivity. Alcoholism was so rife that, according to Boxer in his assessment of both east and west, "it is no exaggeration to say that most of the Dutch and English males who died in the tropics died of drink, even making due allowance for the heavy toll taken by malaria and dysentery."[48] Secondly, religious specialists had to make sure that, among indigenes, the Dutch Reformed faith displaced Roman Catholicism in the many colonies taken over from the Portuguese and the Spanish. Though Calvin, Luther, and the other leaders of the Reformation had been too caught up in domestic religious conflicts to give serious thought to missionary activity outside of Europe, it soon became clear that it would be necessary to challenge the large-scale conversion of colonial peoples already undertaken by the Spanish and the Portuguese in the name of the Pope. In this way the religious conflicts of Europe found their way to the colonies. Thirdly, indigenous religions and their attendant social systems needed to be held in check, as would prove especially difficult for the VOC in the Hindu, Buddhist, and Islamic parts of south and east Asia.

It was difficult for the WIC to keep their employees abroad on the proverbial straight and narrow path of honesty, let alone to maintain their morale. For many, as the saying went, "There were no Ten Commandments south of the Equator."[49] This comment, considered broadly enough to include the Guinea coast, takes on a particularly ironic edge when considered alongside Capitein's translation of the Commandments into Fante: see appendix 1. The deployment of the dregs of Dutch society abroad, the low pay they received, the opportunities for quick enrichment, and the prevalence of smuggling were clearly related factors in the knotty social fabric of West Africa's trading outposts. Matters were not helped by the condescending attitude held by many of the WIC employees toward the indigenes. This was the source of repeated injunctions from the

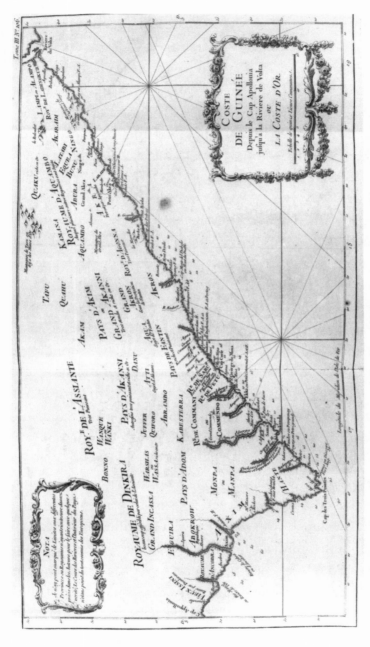

Jacques Nicolas Bellin (1703–1772), *The Coast of Guinea or Gold Coast*, from *Le petit atlas maritime, volume 3* (Paris, 1764). Clements Library, University of Michigan

35

Company to its employees to cultivate good social relations, in the interest of fostering good trade contacts. The real nature of the WIC's motives was made clear by a placard its directors had posted in all of its West African stations in 1722: "Treat all natives with gentleness and friendly words and deeds, in order that they bring their commerce to the company factories ... so that the WIC might benefit."[50] One particular and ongoing concern of both the WIC and the VOC was control over their employees' sexual activities while abroad: the tendency of the Europeans to cohabit with indigenous women was as inevitable as it was troublesome for the two Companies. We have already noted that it was for Capitein a major issue in upholding morals at Elmina, and this may be taken as representative.[51] The aphorism quoted by Boxer, "Necessity is the mother of invention and the father of the Eurasian," was formulated in a VOC context but it applies just as well to the WIC's factories on the Guinea coast as it does to the East Indies.[52]

If the need for Christian mission was there, the difficulties facing its realization were even more overwhelming. It was hard for the WIC and the VOC to find ordained ministers to serve as chaplains (*predikanten*) who were willing and able to accept an overseas station, not surprisingly, given the difficulty in securing even unskilled male personnel from the United Provinces. Those ministers who could adapt to the local conditions tended not to last long before returning home. To make matters worse, the VOC followed the inefficient practice of moving ministers around from

one colony to another after
only a few years. Disaffection
between the *predikant* and the
other Company employees
was a very common phenom-
enon, as is attested in numerous letters from various sides.
The role of the *predikanten*
was supplemented, and in
their absence taken, by lay

Logo of the WIC

readers serving as sick-visitors (*krankbezoekers*) and sick-
comforters (*ziekentroosters*). Humble in status, untrained,
and paid about half an ordained minister's salary, they were
merely allowed to read prescribed texts rather than to pray
or to preach extemporaneously. The tippling tendencies of
these *krankbezoekers* earned them the unflattering nick-
name of "drink-visitors" (*drankbezoekers*).

It is against this background that we should understand
the desire of the WIC leadership to send Capitein back to
Elmina as a missionary in 1742, on terms favorable to itself.
His mission emerges as part of the Company's attempts to
strengthen its position in one of its two remaining strong-
holds. To be sure, the motive of Christian mission is not by
this reckoning completely effaced, but it is set in the all-
important context of mercantile interests. It must not be
forgotten that Capitein's subsequent sojourn in Ghana was
as a paid employee of the WIC, although he was sanctioned
by the Dutch Reformed church as a missionary.[53] By virtue

of this dual allegiance, Capitein's career as a Company-paid missionary speaks volumes for the Netherlands' "strict subordination of church to state—and of God to Mammon."[54]

III. Capitein's writings in overview

1. Missiology

If the bare outlines of Capitein's life are clear, let us consider his writings and thought in greater detail. His earliest work, of which no copies are known to survive, was a treatise entitled "On the calling of the pagans" (*de vocatione ethnicorum*). Nonetheless, the work is summarized by Capitein at the very beginning of the thesis published here. In it he stresses that the process of converting the pagans had begun, but that it was far from complete. The curse that Noah placed on his son Ham (or more particularly on Ham's son Canaan), in a very well-known passage from Genesis, is invoked as a way of underlining the need for the conversion of (African) non-Christians. In brief, the well-worn line of the argument may be summed up as follows: Ham, having seen his father lying naked and drunk, causes his own son Canaan to be cursed by Noah, and with him the peoples of Africa; but the New Covenant of Christianity promises deliverance to all people, even to those under the curse. This has taken place only in part with the coming of Christ, and the final fulfillment is yet to be achieved: this is the role that Christian mission has to play.[55] (This is a problematic story to which we shall return under section IV.1 below.) In any event, Capitein's summary of his earlier work sounds a note of urgency that pervades the dissertation as a whole.

What needs to be noticed even in the summary is Capitein's emphasis on missionary work in Africa. This element of both his academic treatises points toward something that we must regard with the utmost attentiveness: the presence of Capitein's own life in his theology. After all, as was stated above, his entire university education was predicated on his commitment to missionary work. It is the preface of the current treatise that illustrates this connection most explicitly. In referring to his earlier work, "On the calling of the pagans," he stresses repeatedly the burden of evangelization placed on those who are themselves converts to Christianity. The following is what he says just before narrating the course of his life:

> Hence I have always thought that the greatest obligation was placed upon me to be useful to my people at some time. This, I would say, is the greatest obligation, and no injustice. For God, who is to be praised from age to age for the profound richness of his wisdom and foresight, not only led me from Africa to the blessed land of Holland; indeed, he initiated me into a superior religion and endeavored to hand down to me the rudiments of knowledge.

The concerns and approach of the earlier treatise recur

in the work presented here. As I shall illustrate, Capitein's concern with mission and with his own role in converting Africans shines through to an extent that the earlier work predicts. The later work adheres closely to the question posed in its title, namely that of the compatibility of Christianity and slavery. Its notorious conclusion, that the two are indeed compatible, must be understood in the light of the evangelical Protestantism that pervades the work as a whole.

The body of the dissertation, following an introductory chapter which defines slavery, is divided into two parts. The first of these (chapter 2) appeals to the ancient authorities to illustrate that slavery was indeed practiced in Jewish, Greek, and Roman antiquity. Here Capitein cites passages from the Pentateuch (the first five books of the Old Testament) and from Greek and Latin authors including Aristotle, although he criticizes Aristotle's theory of natural slavery. The second, lengthier section (chapter 3) shows Capitein at his full intellectual breadth, using an even wider range of sources to argue the real point of the thesis: that slavery and Christianity are compatible. The final chapter is devoted to two related arguments: the first, that the human spirit and body should be considered separately from each other (sections 1–12), and the second, that Christian doctrine does not stipulate that baptized slaves must be freed (section 13 to the end).

Capitein insists that the Christian faith and slavery can coexist in the moral order. In doing so he falls back upon a centuries-old tradition in which the symbolic and the physical aspects of slavery are distinguished. Complexities of the Christian tradition and the nature of Capitein's use of that tradition will be considered in section IV.1 below, but for the present let us return briefly to Equiano. In his *Interesting Narrative*, he argued openly against slavery on the grounds that it transgressed human worth, and he laid great store in Christianity. In recounting his own life, he speaks of his conversion as an episode on his path to physical freedom. Yet at various points, especially in his letters and speeches, Equiano sometimes tends to the position that slavery was actually a good thing insofar as it made possible the conversion of Africans. To take another example from some twenty years later than Capitein's treatise, the eminent Danish theologian, Erik Pontoppidan (1698–1764), defended the practice of keeping slaves on the grounds that "most of them probably get to know God and his Kingdom better, thereby becoming liberated in Christ, though the servants of men." A radical Protestant of the Pietist persuasion, Pontoppidan wrote of his conviction that "paganism is far worse than the worst degree of Christianity."[56] This theme, expressed on countless occasions but seldom so pointedly, was long to be heard in the arguments of some Christians on behalf of slavery.[57]

The manuscript translated here is without a doubt Capitein's most distinguished work, but it was not his only one. The treatise with which he terminated his schooling at the Hague, "On the calling of the heathen," now lost, has already been mentioned above. Further, Capitein's correspondence with the WIC and with the Classis of Amsterdam can be read in the translation of Kpobi (*Mission in Chains*, appendix). In addition, we should also recognize Capitein's efforts as a translator, for he made three key Christian documents available for speakers of Fante: the Lord's Prayer, the Twelve Articles of Faith, and the Ten Commandments. Capitein's translation of these texts survives. An interesting element of it is its two-part preface. In the first part, Capitein makes clear that the purpose of the translations is practical, namely to make the Christian faith accessible to indigenous and mixed-race schoolchildren of Elmina. It will be remembered that these texts were a major element of the school curriculum. In the modest tone often used in prefaces, he offers the polite disclaimer that "in the course of time it will be refined, so that God will open his door wider to us"; the reason for hesitating, he indicates, is that the Fante language has not yet been completely written down (see appendix 1 below).

This is, in itself, unexceptional. What is remarkable, however, is that this somewhat clichéd preface, in rhetorical terms a standard *captatio benevolentiae* (introductory appeal for the reader's goodwill), is followed by another, distinctly non-standard preface that was written by the publisher, Hieronymus de Wilhem. In it, the publisher casts doubt on the translation offered by Capitein: "The Reverend Mr. Capitein was correct to say in his preface that this translation is not perfect: the observant reader will agree with me that certain words in our [Dutch] language cannot be expressed in the African language [of Fante]." He continues by offering examples. It is clear that he has undertaken the critique by comparing points within the Dutch texts where distinctive words and phrases recur, and then checking these against the Fante versions. In fact, Wilhem admits by implication that he cannot read the Fante translation directly. The author is too far away to be consulted, being now in his second year at Elmina, and the publisher has not been able to find anyone in the Netherlands who is able to read Fante either. Wilhem feels that it is his obligation "to give warning to the reader."

2. A scholar and an African

It is therefore clear that Capitein's translation, useful as it was intended to be, became a problematic issue. This provides us with the spur to think more broadly about the issue of translation: the prefaces of both Capitein and Wilhem make it clear that the difficulties are more than just terminological. They are deeply rooted in culture, with its attendant problems of specificity and comparability. Some significant recent works of scholarship have teased out the considerable cultural issues involved in translating;[58] and it is now widely accepted that every translation is an act of interpretation, since it cannot stand outside the systems of meaning implicit in the languages it seeks to bridge. By this

Portrait of Capitein at the age of 25, published with his dissertation (1742).
Leiden University Library

reckoning, the considerable difficulties that Capitein had in establishing his mission and the school at the Castle of Elmina are emblematic of the wider problems he faced of making himself understood, and even of operating simultaneously, in two different worlds. Such was the nature of the Dutch seaborne empire that these worlds intersected, in those Africans that found their way to the Netherlands, in the WIC employees on the Guinea coast, and not least in the person of Capitein himself.

The visual medium also gives us many clues about how Capitein was viewed. Each of the three portraits of him that are reproduced between the covers of the current edition presents a man who is emphatically both a scholar and an African. His image as a gentleman of polite society is made clear by any comparison with the other male subjects shown here (see pp. 106, 116 and 128 below). The Bible he touches in each case marks him out as a cleric. On the other hand, there is no denying the bodily features that distinguish him from the male subjects of other portraits, in particular dark skin, a flat nose, thick lips and fleshy cheeks. While this combination of features might seem, at first glance, unexceptional, it must be regarded as extraordinary for its time. As Allison Blakely's fine study has shown, Africans were indeed represented in Dutch art of the Golden Age; typically they were portrayed as the servants of wealthy burghers or as caricatures in the decorative arts. Thus the *Portrait of Jan van Amstel and Anna Boxhoorn* by Abraham Lambertsz. van den Tempel (1671) contains,

Portrait of Capitein at the age of 25,
published with Dutch version of dissertation (1742).
Amsterdam University Library

on its right margin, a small black servant whose presence "helps to balance the composition."[59] The scene is typical.[60] What makes the portraits of Capitein exceptional is that they are individualized in a way that is perhaps unmatched by any African in Dutch art up to the mid-1700s.

If the portraits are an indication of how Capitein was considered by his contemporaries, we need to consider the way in which he saw himself; in practice, at least, how he presented himself. First, let us consider the manner in which he indicates his change of status from slave to free. It is worth noting, though it may not be surprising, that Capitein leaves his readers to infer the fact of his manumission from his autobiography. Rather than announcing it explicitly, he marks its place in his narrative with a couplet in honor of Middelburg, the seaport of Zeeland, where he first arrived in Europe:

> This land received me when I first came from Africa,
> and was the door to the vale of the Netherlands.

Comparison with Equiano's passage on his manumission points to the very different character of those two works—and, arguably, also to the difference in their authors' attitudes to slavery. Equiano's narrative at this point is dramatic in its build-up, detail by detail, and packed with overt emotion.[61]

This moment in Capitein's narrative, reinforced by a longer poem on the Hague that follows directly, serves sev-

Portrait of Capitein at the age of 25, after engraving by F. van Bleiswijck,
published with Capitein's dissertation (1742).
Leiden University Library

eral functions at once. Firstly and self-evidently, it express-
es Capitein's sense of divine providence;[62] secondly, it an-
nounces the end of his status as a slave; thirdly and least
obviously, it claims for its author a place among the learned
Dutch aristocracy. If Latin was the scholarly language of the
early modern Netherlands, then the ability to compose
poetry in that language was the mark of learning. Thus, the
treatise as a whole, with its enormous array of scholarly
footnotes, may be regarded as a performance of learning,
and the poems themselves as the *pièce de résistance* of the
treatise. It is poignant to think about the implications of
Capitein's arrival in the Netherlands, and about the elabo-
rateness with which he communicates the significance of
that arrival.

The poem invites comparison with another that was
composed about him by his friend, Brandijn Rijser, on the
eve of his departure. It was published as the caption to a
portrait of Capitein:

> Observer, contemplate this African: his skin is black
> but his soul is white, since Jesus himself prays for him.
> He will teach the Africans faith, hope and charity;[63]
> with him, the Africans, once whitened, will always honor
> the Lamb.[64]

The color-coding of good and evil stretches so far back in
western literary tradition that its earliest origins cannot be
traced. To take one example, the opening lines of the biblical Song of Songs (or Song of Solomon), which dates
back to the 6th century B.C.E., has seemed for generations

of readers to convey this. In the Song the bride says: *I am black and beautiful, O daughters of Jerusalem, like the tents of Kedar, like the curtains of Solomon. Do not gaze at me because I am dark, because the sun has gazed on me.* (1:5–6) This, at least, is the modern translation of the New Revised Standard Version of 1989, accurately conveying the original Hebrew. In effect, however, a strong tendency in the history of the interpretation of this passage has been to see blackness and beauty as adversative, and thus separated by the emphatic conjunction "but" rather than the more neutral "and." Thus the Latin translation in the Vulgate (late 4th century C.E.) has "nigra sum sed formosa," which is later matched by the "I am black but comely" of the King James Version (originally 1611). The point here is not so much the meaning of the original Hebrew passage as the vicissitudes of its interpretation over the centuries.[65] If we accept that the usual interpretation of this passage has generally been an incorrect one (taking "but" for "and"), it is clear that Rijser's poem echoes the color-imagery of the Song of Songs passage; whether directly or indirectly is immaterial for our purposes. The connection is made between blackness and sin, hence the emphasis placed on the conjunction "but" in the Song. The Hebrew poem, in turn, created a new commonplace that is reactivated here by Rijser: that someone can be "black but lovely," in this case lovely in a spiritual sense, as if through a paradox.

Rijser's short dedicatory poem is, to an extent, pure cliché, but, like many clichés, it carries an important message. It points to the somatic encoding of human beings—in a word, of race—in Capitein's world, and in this respect it reflects contemporary Dutch responses to him. The significant point is that the sentiment expressed in the poem resonates with Capitein's ethnological justification for missionary work, namely the attempt to redeem the curse on Canaan in striving to fulfill the covenant.

Capitein, the author of the treatise, was by any reckoning a learned person. His command of scholarly Latin and the truly impressive range of earlier literature to which he appeals leave no room for doubt about this. In the case of Rijser's poem about Capitein, learning was seen as an escape from blackness, just as the beauty of the bride in the Song of Songs is presented in the Hebrew scriptures as an escape from blackness and its web of implications. Such an interpretation of Capitein can be reinforced with reference to his posthumous reputation in the Netherlands.[66]

The work in general, with its florid Latin and ponderous scholarly annotations, and the poems in particular, may be considered public demonstrations of their author's learning, assertions of his place in a social milieu that held scholars and scholarship in high esteem. Capitein's Latin style is particularly elaborate, even for an age steeped in the aesthetics of excess. Its scholarly apparatus of quotes and references is full, and it should be remembered that the composition of Latin poetry carried the special cachet of gentlemanly erudition.[67] The treatise, taken as a whole, reflects the learning that was part and parcel of Reformed sermons of the period.

A brief consideration of the curricula that Capitein would have followed goes a long way toward explaining the process by which he acquired his learning. The Hague Latin school, like other Latin schools of the Netherlands, was an élite institution. Its roots in Dutch humanism were most eminently linked with Erasmus of Rotterdam (ca. 1466–1536) and, beyond that, in Roman Catholic foundations dating back to medieval times. Its emphasis on teaching boys Latin throughout its program and Greek in the senior year remained its distinctive feature, and was part of a commitment to the study of Greco-Roman classical authors and their social background.[68]

Of the Dutch universities, that at Leiden was the oldest, having been established in 1575 by Prince William of Orange to honor the city's heroic resistance to the Spanish siege in the previous year.[69] Its connection with the idea of freedom was obvious from the start, when William wrote in a letter to the States of Holland and Zeeland that it was necessary to establish in their territory a university "to be a firm support to and to maintain freedom and the right and lawful government of the country," where Dutch youth would be "educated and taught in the proper knowledge of God and in all proper, honest and free arts and sciences."[70] The university was therefore from the start a symbol of resistance against Spanish oppression. For much of its subsequent history, Leiden was to remain the Netherlands' most prestigious university, the most international in its professoriate and student body, and the most intimately connected with the nation's overseas enterprise.[71] In the traditional medieval faculties of theology, philosophy, law, and medicine, Latin was the medium of instruction; only in engineering was Dutch used. The most renowned among its many eminent professors was the French-born Joseph Justus Scaliger, who held a research professorship in Leiden from 1593 until his death in 1609. It was under Scaliger's influence that philological studies at Leiden rose to a position of leadership throughout Europe; specifically, he promoted the study of Hebrew and other Semitic languages, in part because of their value to Calvinist theologians in their debates with the Catholics.[72] Hence the presence of Hebrew in the curricula studied by Capitein, and hence a reference to the original Old Testament term for slave in his treatise (ch. 2, sec. 5).

The scholars that Capitein mentions in his treatise were, by and large, theologians, philologists, and jurists of the 17th century. Together they testify to an impressive breadth of learning on his part. A few, such as Augier Ghislain de Busbecq (1522–1592), Jean Bodin (1529–1596), Francis de Ravelinghen (1539–1597), and Johannes Molanus (1553–1585), go back to the 16th century, but these are the minority of those directly cited. For Busbecq, it was wrong for certain peoples to crave physical freedom when in fact they needed leadership to function properly. In this respect he concurred with Bodin's notion of absolute sovereignty, although Bodin himself had attacked the Aristotelian and

Augustinian positions on slavery from an empirical standpoint. Typical of the academic establishment of the early
modern period, the vast majority of scholars combined various spheres of study, particularly legal with theological
studies. This is, in itself, a reminder of the centrality of theology to academic study to a degree that is hard to imagine
in the contemporary western world. Notable examples
are Claude de Saumaise (1588–1653), Johannes Casparus
Suicerus (1620–1684), Paul Voet (1619–1667), and the
enormously influential Dutch jurist, statesman, and theologian, Hugo Grotius (1583–1645). It is in this light that we
are to understand Capitein's institutional background when
he entitles his treatise a "political-theological dissertation."
It is striking that Capitein restricts his specific references to
thinkers with whom he was at least nominally in agreement
on the subject of slavery, whereas none of his "opponents"
or "adversaries" are mentioned by name. As will be discussed below in section IV.2, it is worth noting the polemical tone of his thesis, and Capitein's vivid sense of his
"opponents."

The Enlightenment left a notoriously ambiguous legacy
in the intellectual history of slavery. On the one hand, it
undermined much of the moral authority that had under-
pinned the practice of bondage; it made the institution of
slavery a topic for debate. For example, Voltaire (1694–
1778), an outspoken critic of the Catholic church and
other forms of authority, highlighted the plight of slaves in
Surinam in his widely read novel *Candide* (1758).[73] On the

other hand, a great deal of Enlightenment thought concerning race was far from compassionate. Whereas Montesquieu (Charles-Louis de Secondat, 1689–1755) openly denounced slavery as ethically untenable, as did Jean-Jacques Rousseau (1712–1778), his classically based theory of environmental determinism had, over time, the effect of entrenching racial prejudice against black Africans.[74] The *Encyclopédie*, composed by diverse hands between 1751 and 1780, included both a denouncement of slavery and an extremely negative presentation of blacks.[75] It is unclear how much impact the *philosophes* would have had, by the early 1740s, on Capitein's world. Much of the Enlightenment, arising in the latter part of the century, will not necessarily have had a direct bearing on his position. To be sure, the 18th-century Netherlands were the main center for the publication of writings of the Enlightenment thinkers, as they sought to avoid French censorship.[76] Yet the publication of these works in the Netherlands did not necessarily mean that they were widely read there; certainly we do know that a number of them were banned at the behest of the church. It is as well to bear in mind the broader trends associated with the Enlightenment, for they do indicate that Capitein was on the cusp of large-scale historical change, and that he lived in a transitional period in which anti-slavery sentiment was beginning to gain in volume and breadth.[77] His "opponents," though not named, are therefore a strong presence in his work, dictating its polemical tone and even its careful and wide-ranging scholarship.

This overview of Capitein's scholarly background has shown how its two pillars, namely his Christian education and his classical training, gave him the language with which to defend slavery. But the same texts could easily have been differently deployed to produce other conclusions. It remains for us to consider in broader scope how the Christian tradition harbored various and even contradictory positions on the subject of slavery.[78]

IV. Capitein's dissertation in context

1. A history of Ham's curse: Christianity and slavery

Chattel slavery, it might be said, rests on a central contradiction: that slaves are human, and that they are property. This contradiction was to play out in an astonishing variety of ways within Christian thought alone.[79] An examination of the New Testament and other early Christian writings cannot establish in an unproblematic way that Christianity either condemned or condoned slavery outright. To be sure, the New Testament and the Old include several passages that can be read as endorsements of slavery, but by the same token there are several passages enjoining masters to leniency toward their slaves, notably Paul's letter to Philemon.[80] In the New Testament slavery also serves as a metaphor for subjugation of various kinds: it is possible to be a slave to sin or a slave to Christ.[81] Thus, in an important Pauline passage not cited by Capitein, Christ's sufferings are presented as those of a slave (Philippians 2:6–8).[82] Nor does Capitein mention another passage in which the apostle implies that on earth freedom is preferable to slavery.[83]

Biblical passages on the subject of slavery can be cited and discussed at length, but in a sense, the exact dictates of scripture on the question of slavery are not the point. What matters is the history of their interpretation, even the selectivity with which they are used. To put it differently, a treatise such as Capitein's should be thought of as an appropriation of Christian doctrine in its own right, within a rich and complicated history of exegesis. What is more, various authors citing Christian doctrine appeal either to the chapter-and-verse of scripture, or else to what they perceive as its spirit. For the learned Reformed tradition within which Capitein lived, exegesis was essential to the practice of Christianity, and sermons embodying it formed a basic part of church services, whereas the mass was central to the Catholic tradition critiqued by Calvin. Hence, on the one hand, there was the sense of *sola scriptura*, the idea that the Bible on its own, correctly interpreted, held the key to all questions of doctrine. The Bible was by this reckoning an absolute text.[84] On the other hand, the question of interpretation could at times be a large one, and was recognized as such, given the hermeneutic issues involved. In the case of slavery, this meant the need to make sense of comments from within an early Christian world where slavery was so deeply ingrained in social practice that it was largely taken for granted. The Bible was now expected to help the faithful interpret issues resulting, in part, from the European discovery of a New World.[85]

If all of this is not complicated enough, there are further variables to add to the equation. Most importantly, it is one thing to speak about the doctrinal issues involved at the intersection of slavery and Christianity; it is quite another to consider their practical implications for the traffic in chattel slaves. To take an example from the Americas, the Dominican friar Bartolomé de Las Casas (1474–1566) criticized the harshness with which slaves were treated in South America, but his comments concerned Indian slaves in the first instance.[86] The idea of humanity, defined by possession of a soul, was debated in relation to Indian slaves rather than African. The distinction is an important one, for much of the debate over the rights and wrongs of enslaving South American Indians presupposed the availability of African slaves that were assumed not to be subject to the same criteria of legitimacy. In his apology for slavery as part of a "just war," Juan Ginés de Sepúlveda appealed to the Bible with no less intensity than did his opponent Las Casas, but he argued the opposite case, on the basis of different emphases within the Christian tradition, and consequently he put forth a different interpretation of slavery. In the Iberian colonization of the 15th- and 16th-century New World it was not unknown for missionaries to lend

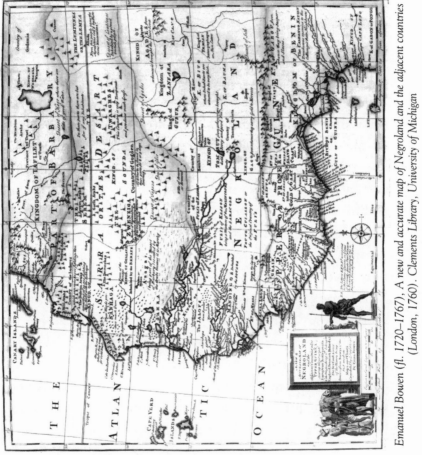

Emanuel Bowen (fl. 1720–1767), A new and accurate map of Negroland and the adjacent countries (London, 1760). Clements Library, University of Michigan

moral support to slavery (as in the case of Sepúlveda), or even to participate actively in it, while they were supposedly engaged in the task of converting the "heathen" to Christianity.[87]

Much of the original impetus of the Reformation involved a direct challenge to the social order, not the least of which was the exploitative position of the Catholic church within that order. For many Protestants the principle of the priesthood of all believers carried a sharp edge of egalitarianism. But some key events soon set the parameters of the Reformed revolution. The Peasants' War led to Luther's composition of the treatise "Against the robbing and murdering hordes of peasants" in 1524, in which he reaffirmed that the world's social hierarchies could not be totally rejected; and the rising in 1534–35 in Munster evinced similar sentiments from other leaders of the Reformation, namely Calvin, Huldrych Zwingli (1484–1531), and Martin Bucer (1491–1551). Thus, from the start there was an ambiguity in Reformed positions relative to the social order, and potentially also to slavery. In its earliest days particularly, the Reformation offered a series of challenges, stemming from a radically egalitarian ethos that stressed the priesthood of all the faithful; on the other hand, once Reformed positions relative to Catholicism began to be strengthened, they were considerably modified on the subject of social hierarchy. This change went hand in hand with the transition from the position of challenger to that of the establishment.

One aspect of Capitein's argument for slavery which seems, in an 18th-century Dutch context, to have a distinctively Calvinist edge was the doctrine of original sin. The concept, which was to be the basis for Calvin's teaching on divine predestination, has its roots in earlier centuries of Christian thought. Augustine in the *City of God* explains slavery as the result of original sin, and by implication defends its existence.[88] For many pro-slavery Protestants, physical freedom was regarded as an undeserved and unexpected boon in the light of original sin, and hence slavery could be regarded as the natural state of humans. Augustine's comments were grist for their mill. Despite some dissenting voices at various points in the history of Christianity, the connection of slavery and original sin was to have the status of orthodoxy until the later 18th century, when the Quakers were among the most outspoken of Christians to oppose slavery on a universal basis.[89] Catholic opposition to slavery reached a high point with the officially sanctioned critique by Nichlas Bergier in 1790. In the case of Capitein, as we gather from the summary of his earlier work, the curse of Ham in effect magnifies the Fall. If the Fall marked the separation of God and man, then slavery represented the most extreme form of man's fallen state. Capitein's presentation of Africans (the "son of Ham") in this light is not new.[90] In the context of Capitein's treatise this color-sensitive version of original sin justifies slavery in so far as it calls for the conversion of the most egregious sinners, black Africans.[91] Free will, although a major part of Protestant thinking generally, plays no part in Capitein's thought. Within his paradigm the efficacy of Christian mission is simply assumed.

One notable absence among Capitein's sources is that of Johannes Coccejus (1603–1669), Professor of Theology at Leiden from 1650 until his death. His work on missiology, which brought him into conflict with the Utrecht-based Gisbertus Voetius (1589–1676), was very influential, particularly in theological studies at Leiden. Whereas Voetius, true to orthodox Calvinism, emphasized the doctrine of election in his missiology, Coccejus spoke of mission in the context of a covenantal progression leading from the garden of Eden to the second coming of Christ. Much of Christian mission over the long centuries of its history has been explicitly eschatological in its impetus, in other words, impelled by an urgent sense of the imminent second coming.[92] The Netherlands of the early 18th century was to prove especially receptive to this line of thinking. For the Pietists especially, concern with the impending afterlife determined the immediate need for mission. Coccejus' conception of Christian mission included a practical side, complete with directives on the kind of language to be employed, but it was based on the notion of the approaching end of the world. Ham's curse was to play a prominent role in Coccejus' writings, linked with Calvin's doctrines of election and predestination.

In contrast to Coccejus, Capitein's missiology, at least as expressed in this treatise, was far from practical. He merely assumed that missions would be successful; his idea of mission was intimately bound up with the slave trade. Indeed, if his concern for mission drove him to accept slavery, then he was not in a position to express any doubt as to the intimacy of the connection between the two. The treatise gives the impression that he was more concerned with masters than with slaves, but this slant may of course be seen as a function of the social context of the treatise and its intended audience. There is no indication within it of any premonition of the problems, either broadly cultural or narrowly logistic, that beset his ministry. There is also no hint in the treatise of the basic difficulty of translating the important Christian texts into a native language, a practical difficulty that was to cause him to produce the text referred to in Appendix 1 below.

In its more abstract forms, the influence of Coccejus' theology on Capitein's missionary outlook is explained by its enduring presence at Leiden, in particular the teaching of Henrik Velse, who was a formative influence on the youthful Capitein. This much Capitein says in his preface. Velse, himself trained at Leiden in the years 1699–1707, never held an academic chair of theology, but in his writings and sermons strongly advocated the spread of the gospel among non-Christians. In his preface to the "Detailed reports on the establishment of Christendom among the heathen on the Coromandel and Malabar coasts" (*Naauwkeurige berigten nopens de grondvesting van het christendom onder de heiden op de kust van Choromandel en*

Malabar), published in 1739, he holds up the Danish missionaries based at Tranquebar as a shining example to all Protestants.[93] Capitein in fact mentions the work, and especially Velse's preface to the Dutch translation, in the final chapter of his treatise. The Herrnhutters or Moravians, a Pietistic branch of the Lutheran church, are also praised by Velse for the zeal with which they approach their task of evangelizing the heathen. Velse stressed the missionary's need to learn the language of the people evangelized, and emphasized the catechetical teaching of the young. He was explicitly aware of the problems involved in preaching to and converting slaves. Against the objection that the conversion of slaves would lead to social instability, he counters that it would in fact make slaves more honest and thus enhance both economic viability and social interaction. Most importantly, Velse explicitly argues that owners are under no obligation to free converted slaves.[94]

Capitein devotes the concluding chapters of the dissertation to this last issue. Within the plan of the treatise this matter is tackled as the final notional obstacle to the pursuit of Christian mission: the possibility that its success would undermine the entire slave system, whose Christian legitimacy and existence in long-term history are both proven by this point of the work. In arguing a position close to that of Velse, Capitein focuses on the institution of *manumissio in ecclesia*, the practice of freeing converted slaves, begun by the Christian emperor Constantine (r. 306–37) in the year 321 C.E. In practice Constantine was giving the churches special power to manumit slaves, provided that the bishop was present.[95] Capitein's argument is that this *manumissio* was inspired not by divine law but rather by specific circumstances, and that hence it carries no implications for the present time. In short, slave-owners have nothing to fear from the conversion of their slaves.

As a broad generalization, it might be said that until the 18th century, the concept of slavery was interpreted by Christians in a metaphorical or symbolic rather than physical way. This is certainly a feature of many of the theoretical discussions of slavery, at least up to the Enlightenment. The Synod of Dordt (1618–19) may be considered a new departure, for it undoubtedly represented the start of a process by which the moral legitimacy of slavery began to be whittled down. Although it did not take a firm line on the practice of slavery, it left the task of deciding to individual slave owners. The process was a slow one, and was not to produce substantial results until the later 18th century. Seen against this background, Capitein's theology appears, at best, a product of its times, and particularly of the 17th-century tradition with which he effectively identifies himself. At worst, it appears conservative at a period of broader change, notably the loss of status by the Dutch trading empire, and the growing impact of Enlightenment thinkers. Certainly, much of the work reaffirms an older, pre-abolitionist tendency to interpret slavery in a non-physical way. Capitein in his treatise does not mention who exactly he is arguing against, but it is clear that he is participating in an ongoing debate. This in itself suggests the presence of abolitionist thought well ahead of the later 18th century.

The name of Christianity, complete with chapter-and-verse citations from its scripture, was invoked over many centuries in defense of slavery *per se*, and, paradoxically, in arguments for leniency in its application. Capitein himself argues that it is not just for a master to treat his slave harshly: "We readily concede that Christian charity does not permit Christians to brutalize their slaves" (ch. 3, sec. 23). Much of the debate on the moral legitimacy of slavery may thus be said to have occurred within the parameters of Christian doctrine. No less than the Quakers arguing the opposite position, Capitein's treatise shows Christian doctrine providing the entire framework of the debate over legitimacy. But in the case of Capitein, it was a kind of Christianity that placed the greatest store on missionary activity, and as a result defended the legitimacy of slavery.

2. Antislavery sentiment in the Netherlands

It would be wrong to give the impression that the debate about slavery in the Netherlands was decided entirely within the parameters of Christian theology. We have already seen that the issue of the legitimacy of slavery was raised at the time of the establishment of the WIC, and hence the complex interplay of ethical and commercial concerns.

Clearly, various factors need to be considered together.

In a major contribution to the study of Dutch antislavery sentiment, Seymour Drescher had this to say: "The prerevolutionary period in the Netherlands produced only the faintest echoes of hostility toward slavery in the form of Latin treatises, anonymous poems, and occasional poems."[96] These represented no more than "isolated expressions hardly noticed by the general public."[97] It is true that the 18th century did see critiques of the Dutch seaborne empire, but that was not until its closing decades. An important literary work deserves mention here, as it is arguably the first Dutch work to represent the colonial presence in the Caribbean in an unfavorable light: Elisabeth Maria Post's *Reinhart, of natuur en godsdienst* ("Reinhart, or nature and religion": Amsterdam, 1791–92), a novel written in the form of letters. It did not appear until five decades after Capitein's treatise, and has been seen as a text of the Enlightenment.[98]

However, we see in the treatise translated here that Capitein himself noticed and responded to criticisms of slavery as early as 1742. Unfortunately for modern-day scholars, he does not mention these "opponents" by name, and in the process it is harder to know exactly who he is referring to. With all of this in mind, let us return briefly to the "adversaries" Capitein mentions in his treatise: vestigial though they are, they may prove to be the key to understanding the intellectual landscape that he inhabited. A renewed attempt must be made to identify and analyze them in the light of antislavery sentiment in the Netherlands.

As early as 1615 the Dutch comic poet Gerbrand Adriaenszoon Bredero published a play called *Moortje* ("Little Moor"), in which reference is made to the trade in slaves by merchants from Amsterdam. The work contains an explicit condemnation of the trade, most notably at the following lines, which are spoken by a merchant from Amsterdam:

> Inhumane custom! Godless rascality!
> That people are being sold, to horselike slavery.
> In this city also there are those who engage in the trade.
> [This trade occurs] in Farnabock, but God will know.[99]

Given the early date of the work, before even the establishment of the WIC, it has been surmised that it refers to the slaving activities of Sephardic Jews, who had centuries earlier emigrated to Amsterdam from Portugal, yet they traded with the Portuguese in Pernambuco in Brazil.[100] If this analysis is correct, the reference brings more complication than clarity to the picture of Dutch antislavery sentiment since it involves anti-Semitic feeling at the same time.

Now it is true that the Netherlands, compared with other western European states, did not show antislavery leanings until late. This historical fact has been the subject of an engaging recent debate; in particular, it has intensified comparative perspectives on the study of antislavery sentiment.[101] The disparaging witticism attributed to the German writer Heinrich Heine (1797–1856) has been invoked as a comment on the phenomenon: "If the world were to come to an end, I would go to Holland, where everything happens fifty years later."[102]

Much of this debate centers on the difficulty of identifying the economic issues underlying the antislavery movement, when the economic viability of slavery is now widely accepted by scholars. Contrary to earlier trends, it is no longer possible to explain the decline of slavery in terms of profitability: it is simply not the case that slavery was abolished because it failed to benefit slave-owners financially. The belatedness of Dutch antislavery thinking is therefore a problem of historical analysis, given the economic prosperity of the Netherlands in the 17th century, and given its capitalist development which anticipated that of France and Britain. Drescher has stressed that Britain and the Netherlands took different paths in relation to economic development and antislavery feeling, and that the British case should be seen as anomalous rather than paradigmatic.[103]

The debate is a complicated one, and it leaves us, for current purposes, to consider its relevance to Capitein and his treatise. The debate over antislavery thought helps us to find his place in the intellectual world of the Netherlands particularly; it helps us to see his status as a slave-turned-freedman within the history of Dutch slavery. If we are to characterize Capitein's fifteen years in the Netherlands prior to the publication of this treatise, we might say that they were lived within the period of "fifty years," to use Heine's evocative, if approximate, designation. Antislavery sentiment was rife in many parts of Europe. More to the point perhaps, Capitein's treatise shows us that his was an age when there were opposing voices on the subject of slavery. Indeed, the work, with its references to the antislavery "adversaries," suggests that the supposed fifty years of Dutch belatedness may be something of an exaggeration. Capitein offers both explicit and implicit indications of antislavery sentiment in the Netherlands, both in the references to his unnamed "adversaries" and in the overall polemical thrust of his treatise. His text presented here thus calls for a rethink of Drescher's analysis, or at least suggests some measure of qualification.

Shortly before the WIC was chartered in 1621, the momentous Synod of Dordt (November 1618–May 1619) took place. This assembly of the Reformed Church discussed and eventually rejected the challenge brought by the Remonstrants, a group that followed the teachings of Jacobus Arminius on the subject of predestination.[104] The Synod's doctrinal decisions would shape the thought of the Reformed Church up to the present day. While it brought neither a universal condemnation nor legitimization of slavery, it left its acceptability up to individual burghers to decide. As an arbitration, this was clearly a compromise between opposing positions; yet it does attest to the presence of antislavery sentiment in the Netherlands. Thus it happened that slaves travelling to the Netherlands after 1648 were subject to implicit metropolitan manumission, which is how Capitein attained his freedom.

Two factors may be seen behind the decision of the Synod, and indeed underlying the existence of Dutch anti-slavery sentiment. Firstly, the concept of "freedom" carried considerable weight in the Netherlands at and after the time of the Spanish hegemony. In the revolt against Spain in 1568 freedom was a rallying cry of the Dutch leader, William the Silent. He was claiming not to be setting up a separate state but seeking liberty of conscience and civic autonomy in matters of law and order. The Spaniards, after all, had moral legitimacy on their side.[105] In a different register, a notable occurrence of the concept of freedom is to be found in Hugo Grotius' *Mare liberum* (1633), which argues for free trade and thus provides moral justification for the Netherlands' seaborne empire in the Indian Ocean. Freedom was a many-splendored thing, prevailing at different levels and in different ways in the minds of early modern Netherlanders: what it meant in practice, however, was not always as clear.[106] Descartes, for one, expressed his disappointment that the Dutch Republic, once freed from the shackles of Spanish rule, had not realized the ideal of freedom in a meaningful way. As Drescher rightly points out, "true freedom" (*waare vrijheid*) remained in this period a political concept with no particular implications in labor relations.[107] The critical problem for the historian today is thus to identify the practical implications of the concept, in this case regarding the status of labor. In fact, there are good reasons to imagine that there was no explicit equation made between the more notional political sense and the narrow civic sense, affecting the lives of foreigners at home or abroad. It is thus clear that the concept of freedom was deployed on a selective basis in the slave-trading society of the Dutch seaborne empire.

Secondly, a strong philanthropic streak ran through Dutch society in the 17th century. This was manifested in the widespread establishment of hospices and poorhouses, which so stuck in the minds of foreign travelers to the Netherlands. The College of Aalmoezeniers (almoners), founded in 1613 to deal with the growing number of poor in Amsterdam, is merely one example, but a famous one. Indicative of this trend, the British ambassador at the Hague, Sir William Temple, records that, on his travels in the Dutch hinterland, an aged former seaman refuses his gift of a coin. When Temple insists on making the donation, the seaman passes it on to a small child. Amazed at the good provision made for the Dutch poor, Temple notes soberly that "charity seems to be very national among them."[108] As Schama's *Embarrassment of Riches* has extensively shown, the accumulation of wealth on the part of Dutch burghers was accompanied by a complex set of reactions, not least of which was a strong humanitarian impulse to work to improve the lot of society's outcasts, including Gypsies, other foreigners, and prostitutes. What Schama does not mention, however, is the extent to which Africans may have benefited from such efforts. The implications of this for Capitein's life, therefore, must remain open to some degree. It is clear from the work of Schama and others that kindness was a striking feature of social life in the Netherlands, and in fact played a major part in the self-presentation of Dutch burghers.[109]

V. Conclusions

Defining slavery: ownership and social death

The definition of slavery offered in the first chapter of Capitein's treatise proper presents, however improbably, a good note on which to conclude these introductory comments. In beginning his discussion of the topic of the thesis, Capitein distinguishes slavery from all voluntary forms of dependency, that is to say "servant" status, preferring instead the juridical definition of "a status in which someone is unwillingly subjected to the authority of another." In so far as Capitein's definition focuses on ownership, it accords with that expounded in modern times by Moses Finley, a scholar whose insights on both ancient and comparative slavery continue to provide a point of departure.[110] Much of Capitein's thesis reveals a tendency to move conceptually between physical slavery, the prime subject of Finley's attention, on the one hand and the metaphorical realm on the other. Such vacillation is not a new or an unusual thing, and can be widely instantiated from within the biblical and Greco-Roman traditions of antiquity. Seen in this light, Capitein's brief introductory definition offers little difficulty.

But if the Finleyite concept of slavery resonates with Capitein's explicit definition, then it is another which is brought into focus by his life story. In his influential book, Orlando Patterson has characterized slavery in terms of "social death"—a deracination of social context which is, self-evidently, truer of some forms of subjugation than it is of others. For Patterson this is a radical non-belonging and marginality, typically originating in and even sustained by violence.[111] Capitein's autobiography offers no more than a few sentences on his brief life as a slave, sold first to the seaman Arnold Steenhart and then handed over to the merchant Jacob van Goch. Yet even in these few lapidary sentences, violence lurks not far from view: "As a boy of seven or eight, orphaned by war or some other cause . . . " Capitein does however offer considerable detail about his life in the Netherlands.

It is far more Capitein the freedman than Capitein the slave that is presented to us in his autobiography. This, it may be countered, is unsurprising in the context of a scholarly work and in the context of Capitein's social world, at a time when the abolitionist movement had not yet gained much momentum. True though it may be, such a concession does not absolve us from questions about Capitein's social standing in the Netherlands during his sojourn there in the years from 1726 to 1742. To put it bluntly: to what extent was Capitein's life in the Netherlands a time of "social death"? The question may sound perverse, given the fact that, in the formal sense, Capitein gained his freedom on arriving in Middelburg. In the most obvious respect, the gratitude to Van Goch and other patrons expressed in the preface is echoed in his letters to the WIC from Elmina. Various poems to and from Dutch friends, as in section III.2 above, may be cited.

But this is not the entire story. Was the social proximity expressed by Capitein more a matter of wishful thinking than an actuality? The question should remain open, given that our perspective on Capitein's time in the Netherlands is based so much on his own comments. It is certainly possible that the circumstances of his life were more isolated than he suggests, that much of the kindness he received shaded into patronizing behavior; and consequently that he, though not formally subject to chattel slavery, was in some very real senses "socially dead." At issue here is the degree of integration into Dutch society Capitein experienced, and this is by nature a topic about which it is easier to speculate than it is to form hard-and-fast conclusions. To be sure, his later falling out with the company and the Classis suggests the tenuousness of his situation as a client, and hints that his status of relative privilege and acceptance depended ultimately on his ability to satisfy Dutch mercantile interests. In particular, the circumstances surrounding his marriage suggest that his relationship with the WIC was marked by a substantial degree of unfreedom. The initiative of the Directors in sending Capitein a "suitable" wife of their own choosing underlines their ongoing power over him, and the long arm of the Dutch seaborne empire is thus seen at full stretch.

*   *   *   *   *   *

If the dissertation offered here represents the meeting of Western theory and African experience, it is a strange meeting which leaves several questions unanswered. To put the cat among the pigeons, it is even possible that a note of irony pervades the treatise. This would explain why, for example, Capitein has such a strong sense of his "adversaries" and gives them such strong arguments from start to finish; and why he himself opposes Aristotle's theory of natural slavery. It must be remembered that the 18th century was an age in which satire flourished in various literary genres. In short, the suggestion is not as outlandish as it might seem initially.

Even without pursuing this intriguing possibility, the questions of interpretation multiply if Capitein's life is considered alongside his treatise, as indeed it should be. Most pressingly, from a modern standpoint: what motivated a former slave to defend slavery, in the name of Christianity? What was the level of Capitein's social integration or isolation in the Netherlands? Most tellingly, if we try to grasp his inner life: did Capitein participate in the slave trade himself, and if so, under what circumstances? Some answers have been hinted at in the paragraphs above, but these can never be more than provisional and speculative. Even when documentary evidence does survive, we are left to read between the lines. Capitein the person remains much more elusive to us today than does Capitein the scholar.

Thus a significant level of uncertainty clouds any conclusions reached, but it might still be worthwhile to offer an overall assessment, even if that can only be a tentative one. Ultimately, it seems, it is the imperative of Christian mission that most informs Capitein's treatise. It might be argued, to a greater extent than Kpobi allows, that this in itself was part of the commercial impetus. It is also possible that Capitein, once he had returned to Elmina, himself became involved in trade activities, but this need not be the decisive point in an assessment of his life and thought. The priority that evolved with his years of education at the Hague and Leiden—his mission in two senses—was the conversion of Africans, and his arguments effectively supporting slavery must be seen as contributing to this end. Even making provision for too much retrojection on the part of modern historians, it is impossible to ignore the prominence of Christian mission in Capitein's life, in the various forms it took, from his schooling at the Hague to his death at Elmina.

By this analysis it is beside the point to write Capitein off as an "Uncle Tom," even though the practical implications of his treatise do tally with the interests of his Dutch masters and patrons. Capitein's goals as expressed in the treatise did overlap with those of the WIC in that both condoned or promoted the slave trade. This much is clear.

However, the analysis of Capitein's life and his world offered above point to a different emphasis. He has been presented here as an active campaigner for the conversion of Africans, and a courageous one at that. The treatise promotes conversion in the first instance, and accepts slavery as a necessary and even convenient means to that end, a means that was found throughout ancient societies: in this sense it was legitimized by the past for life in the present and the future. It would be a willful and inaccurate reading of the treatise to imagine that it sought in the first instance to justify slavery when the goal of Christian conversion is so clearly at its core.

The picture that remains from a reading of the work is that of a man who devoted his considerable learning to the spreading of Christianity—and, ultimately, to the interests of his patrons in the WIC, and of the slave trade. The story of Capitein points to the process by which a slave-system could perpetuate itself despite burning questions about its moral legitimacy; it points to a process by which servitude could co-opt one of its victims, perhaps even actively. In these senses it is neither an exaggeration nor undue sensationalism to speak of the agony of Asar.

JACOBUS ELISA JOHANNES CAPITEIN

Political-theological dissertation examining the question:
Is slavery compatible with Christian freedom or not?

PREFACE: To the Reader

More than four years have elapsed since I composed a thesis *On the calling of the heathen* with all my youthful strength, having passed on from the schools of the Hague to attending academic lectures. I divided the work into three parts, as follows:

Chapter I: The promises made concerning Japheth and Ham are found in the occupations of their descendants, according to God's true word.[112]

Chapter II: Although the calling of the heathen is referred to in the New Testament, one must nevertheless understand that it was actualized only in part, even though its full extent was anticipated.

Chapter III: Given that it was anticipated, in what ways will it arrive? Also in the third chapter, as the main theme, I consider how God has been so long entreated with persistent prayers to allow his word, joined with abundant gifts of the Holy Spirit, to be proclaimed to those heathen who have never heard of his name till the present day.

Next, I divided into four parts those very means by which, if scrupulously followed, this task which is pleasing to God can be undertaken and promoted. The first stresses the necessity of understanding those languages by which we may encourage the heathen to convert to Christianity. The second asks that, when those tribes are approached, a suitable place be established for holding meetings. The third section shows that an intimate relationship with them must be sought at all costs, so that while they learn of that delightful sweetness of Christian brotherhood, they are drawn into it. Finally, since all these things cannot be accomplished without teachers, the fourth section places great emphasis on the need to train teachers and send them to the heathen—I mean those endowed with particular learning and piety, strangers to avarice and tyranny, so that they do not frighten away the unfortunate people by the harshness of their authority, but persuade them in a gentle and kind spirit. Now, since I shall shortly complete the course of my academic studies, by the grace and aid of the most high God, I shall try in this preface to introduce the topics I was then speaking about.

(1) In general, it is incumbent on all true Christians to promote diligently those means which enable this conversion of heathen, God willing, to develop, whether independently or with the help of others.

(2) In particular, the task has been entrusted to those who are linked to this or that tribe, from which they themselves were converted to Christianity. This is found to be the situation when converts devote themselves to missionary work.

On the whole, nobody will deny Christian truths when

viewed in this way. For since those people all accomplish with perseverance and joy the religious work which is most pleasing to God, they are bound and obliged to recognize of their own accord that this burden is forced on them—provided that they scrutinize closely and fairly the nature of the New Covenant, and the burning eagerness of the Apostles and missionaries to this purpose, and finally the times in which we live.[113] This is one of the features by which the New Dispensation is distinguished from the Old, and should by no means be criticized, namely that worship of God must no longer be restricted to one place or one race. This has all been foretold for you in the books of the prophets. Firstly, Hosea said (2:23): *I will say to those who were not my people, "You are my people,"* and Joel (2:28): *Then afterward I will pour out my spirit on all flesh.* In fact Peter, filled with the Holy Spirit, applied each promise to our current situation in the most eloquent words.[114] But above all, we must not overlook the words of Zechariah, who said (14:9): *On that day the lord will be one and his name one.*[115] The cause of all this is that the Messiah, about to be sent to the world at that time, after sacrificing his own soul for the guilty, would receive from his father an enormous kingdom extending to the farthest shores of the world. This is how, to adopt a loftier tone, the Psalmist depicts the glory of this kingdom, the citizens and the frontiers in vivid colors, and sings of the Messiah with resounding voice: *May he have dominion from sea to sea, and from the river to the ends of the earth,* etc. (Psalm 72:8).[116]

And so, once he had come to earth at the predicted time, he placed the seat of his spiritual kingdom at the mountain of Holy Zion, where all the Jews who were awaiting the consolation of Israel had been stationed. But, as he continually stressed to those who heard him, he wanted this to take place through the spirit and through truth, among the people and in the land where God is worshipped in the New Dispensation. He sent his disciples to preach not only throughout the entire land of Israel, but he also wished them to approach all nations without distinction. Those who were obedient to the word of their lord and king boldly scorned all life-threatening dangers, and gladly gave up their possessions so as to inspire all and sundry to the faith, until the majority of people entered the spiritual kingdom of Christ and all Israel was saved. In fact there was so much zeal among the apostles that one would try to outdo the rest in performing this duty. It is more than sufficient to observe Barnabas and Paul, whose description in the Bible overflows with great and everlasting praise, since they are called *men who have risked their lives for the sake of our lord Jesus Christ* (Acts 15:26). The followers gladly stood by the rest of the Apostles, although the anger of the enemies of truth and various torments were cast upon them—people such as Timothy, Titus, Clement of Rome, Polycarp of Smyrna, Quadratus, Ignatius and others, whose history William Cave and other scholars have written.[117]

Who that is already a Christian and in whose innermost

spiritual thoughts this name carries a profound meaning, as is fitting, would not wish to imitate those founders of the assembly of Christ who were very pleasing to God?—especially in our day and age when the church is no longer harassed on all sides as once it was, but now that a wide doorway is opened up so that the mysteries of the Gospel may be known even by people across the seas, people who have until this day been enveloped in the darkest cloud of ignorance, and who have not been reached by God's word. Indeed, those who by God's wondrous prudence and goodness converted from paganism to Christianity can be of use in spreading the Gospel, and should in fact commit themselves to this endeavor. For apart from the fact that nature itself of its own accord says to all people that they should strive first of all to do good to those people who are joined to them by a closer bond, it is clear from the mission work of the apostles that, before they traveled to pagan tribes to proclaim the gospel, they needed to take care of the well-being of their own people, the Jews, according to the command of the Lord himself (Matthew 10:6).[118] Hence I have always thought that the greatest obligation was placed upon me also to be useful to my people at some time. This, I would say, is the greatest obligation, and no injustice. For God, who is to be praised from age to age for the profound richness of his wisdom and foresight, not only led me from Africa to the blessed land of Holland; indeed, he initiated me into a superior religion and endeavored to hand down to me the rudiments of knowledge. No Christian will begrudge me a few words here as I set forth a summary, so that I can describe God's providential care for me and my studies.

As a boy of seven or eight, orphaned by war or some other cause, I was sold to admiral Arnold Steenhart, who had landed at a certain place in Africa called St. Andrew's River in order to buy slaves. That eminent man returned when I recently spent time in Middelburg.

After traveling from there to the Castle, the citadel of Elmina, and then on to Shama, he gave me to his friend, Jacob van Goch, now my greatly revered patron and Maecenas,[119] someone who will have my filial affection right up to the grave. At that time he was a very successful and skillful merchant on behalf of the noble directors of the African Society. He wanted me to be known as Capitein ("Captain") and he doted on me with paternal love thanks to his good character which caused his fame to spread virtually throughout all Guinea.[120] Eventually, when he was about to return to his native land, he promised that he would take me with him and would see to it that after being duly instructed in Christianity, I might practice some trade which was not demeaning and thereby earn a living. After some years, in the course of which the acclaimed admiral sailed back from Zeeland to Guinea, miraculously guided by God, we sailed over and arrived at Middelburg in Zeeland. This event I have described elsewhere with the following verse:

This land received me when I first came from Africa
and was the door to the vale of Holland.

Later we proceeded from this city and made for the Hague, birthplace of my honored patron:

> This is the place where our sequestered youth
> was devoted to noble studies.
> This is where Holland's forefathers came
> and met to save the pact of nourishing peace.
> This place with a thousand roads and shady retreats
> fosters ease and lays cares aside.

In this most delightful Dutch town I not only learned the rudiments of the Dutch language but I also worked on the art of painting, in which I proved to be quite talented. Meanwhile, with the passage of time, a most humane person called Johann Philipp Manger allowed me to join the catechists at his private institute. I always stood out as an admirer of this man, who had a sound education and a singular devotion to God, and upon his journey to the mournful fates, when he was taken from the church of the Hague last year, I composed the following mournful elegy:

> Hostile death brandishes its spear throughout the world
> and forces everyone to succumb.
> Fearless it penetrates the halls of kings
> and even gives orders to those who hold power.
> It does not allow rulers to contemplate the triumphs
>   they have won
> but forces them to abandon their opulent trophies.
> It claims for itself all the treasures of the rich,
> and even the cottage of the poor, and divides it among others.
> With its sickle it reaps together young and old
> without distinction, like grains of corn.

Veiled in a black shroud it dared
to disturb the threshold of Manger's house.
When the dismal cypresses stood before his home
noble Hague groaned balefully.
His dear wife soaked him with her tears
and repeatedly beat her breast with her hand.
Just so did Naomi pour forth tears
once widowed by your death, Elimelech.[121]
The sorrowful wife kept pleading with the shades of the dead
and wailing in a tearful voice,
while Phoebus buried his face in a black veil
to deny the land its beloved sunshine.
O my immortal glory, my only delight!
So you flee from my sight and leave me wounded.
Husband, I would not mind if a swift breeze
has carried you to a joyful home in heaven.
But whenever I urge peace and quiet on my limbs,
or when day comes, I remember you still.
Death snatched you away from our marriage-bed.
What day will renew our broken bonds?
Look how your sacred home, dedicated to studies,
now bears the marks of gloomy sorrow for you.
The dear children of our marriage-bed
shed tears flowing as from a brimming stream.
The tender sheep are scattered as if their loyal shepherd
has been wretchedly torn apart by wolves' teeth.
Their shuddering bleats rend the air
when they spot their tattered leader and call out to him.
Thus we fill our halls with plaintive cries
while your corpse lies empty on the bed.
The pious throng joins with your mournful widow
who marks the funeral in a suitable way.

This great jewel of priests, my glory, comes to an end,
the Lord's delight, beloved of good folk.
His sweet mouth is closed, which was fed
by a sacred font with which I relieved my thirst.
Alas, how suddenly fled that eloquence
which I enjoyed as heavenly nectar.
You ancient poets laud the eloquence of Nestor,
but Manger was greater than Nestor himself.[122]
He disturbed the demon of the Styx with his powerful words
as he entered the house, O Christ our leader.[123]
From death he called back souls about to die
and asked Christ to substitute his own neck.
In shining form he showed me salvation
and taught me the way of justice.
Through prayer he put my wishes before God's throne
and the Lord heard his fervent prayers.
His eyes which shone like a yellow lightning flash
now stand stiff, oppressed by eternal quiet of sleep.
Like a scout in heaven, with his eyes he has laid aside
the evil darts thrown by the devil.
A bloodless, pale look occupies his gentle face
where there was once charm mixed with severity.
Likewise is his forehead pale,
which was often touched by grim winter's cold.
If anyone recounts more, great sadness overruns their limbs
as they try to address final words to this man:
Honored father, though we are burying you, a second part
of you which will not die climbs up to Mount Olympus.[124]
Surely some rejoicing will do your soul no harm,
since you take to the shades a just reward of the sacred fight.
Surrounded by soft linen among the denizens of heaven
you are now fed, as victor, with ambrosial food.[125]

With rejoicing soul, drink from the glassy stream
water springing forth from the soil.
No day will ever be able to disturb your peace;
death is overcome and lies beneath your feet.
These very things were taught by your most recent
    words, father,
to a holy throng listening with open ears.

The providence of the wise Lord concerning the pursuit of my studies at the catechistic school of the great and blessed theologian must be broached, if not exhaustively then at least for the most part. Among the catechists I became acquainted with the two generous sons of Willem Henrik van Schuylenburch, who at the time were purported to have said to one of the sons of Henrik Velse, an eminent theologian, that they thought I should steer my career-path toward the study of theology, so that, God willing, I might afterwards show my people the way to a better religion, since they need to be diverted from their cult of idolatry. Now I admit that I do not clearly remember whether I disclosed to anyone that such an idea appealed to me. But it is true that this theologian, for his part, being always very eager to spread the gospel, summoned me and asked whether the report was true. I replied that I certainly did not shrink from the proposal. Then he went to my most esteemed patron and asked whether he wished to send me to the public schools. From that time on he set aside his own funds for me, not only for the liberal arts, but he also supplied as generously as possible whatever was required for the proper pursuit of academic studies.

The Library of Leiden University: engraving by Willem Swanenburgh
after a drawing by Jan Cornelisz. Woudanus, 1610. Leiden University Library

At that time the school superintendent was one Isaac Valkenaar, someone widely known for his scholarly intellect. Whenever I summon up his memory, I can visualize even now his extremely devoted support for me to be educated privately. When all this happened, I became known through the memorable theologian Henrik Velse, to F. C. Roscam, a noblewoman of immense endowments, who greatly helped me in learning Latin and then taught me the rudiments of Greek, Hebrew, and Chaldean.[126] She is dedicated to unblemished piety and to the study of languages, and she makes her house available to young students without charge. She also afforded my education no small advantage in that she introduced me to the influential and noble Peter Cunaeus: to him and to the rest of my patrons I have dedicated this dissertation, for what it is worth. When I was moved up from the first to the fourth class I received holy baptism from J. Philipp Manger in a service held by Ludwig Timon Pielat, whose outstanding rhetorical skill as well as his study of Practical Theology, as it is called, deservedly cause listeners of all ranks to hang on his words. At that point I was named Jacob after my esteemed patron, Elisa after his sister, who has been like a second mother to me, and Johannes after their cousin, who is the wife of Peter Nesker, a very successful clerk and chief secretary. And so for six years, with half my schooling completed and a public oration delivered under the guidance of the rector, Rutger Ouwens, a man steeped in both of the learned languages, I was sent to this most distinguished of Holland's universities. Since the costs to be paid for anyone's academic studies to be completed properly were not small, the most honorable curators of the University of the Hague and the most eminent senators of Holland graciously bestowed their patronage on me, so that after being trained in the liberal arts I could at last bury myself completely in theology. Since all of this has come to pass, full of wonder I burst forth with these appropriate words of the psalm (39[40]:6): *How wondrous are your works, God, how precious to me are your plans! How manifold is the universe!*

For the reasons stated above, the gospel must be spread in our time wherever the dominion and power of Christians are open to it. Nevertheless I have often come to the realization that some Christians fear that through evangelic freedom slavery will disappear entirely from those colonies which Christians own, to the great detriment of the overseers of those colonies. Indeed there were once, and still are, people in the Christian world, and especially in the Netherlands, who, led astray by some unknown spirit, have determined that evangelic freedom cannot coexist with servitude of the body. As I shall demonstrate, my own present situation demands that I prove that such an opinion stems either from ignorance about the nature of evangelic doctrine, or from superstitious anxiety stemming from the customs of the early Christians, or finally from the institutions and morals of these regions.

God, favor these youthful undertakings
and let my words not detract from your praise.
Holy one, you condemn people's foul lies,
and vain superstition does not smile at you.
While I follow the shining trail of truth
may you always lead me along the right path.

CHAPTER ONE,
which defines slavery and proposes
the subject of inquiry

Scholars applaud Cicero's dictum that "every argument about something which is rationally undertaken should proceed from a definition so that it is understood what is being disputed" (*On duties* 1.7).[127] For this reason we shall define slavery before beginning to speak. We do not perceive slavery to involve any voluntary agreement, whereby two or more persons mutually pledge that one person will act as a slave in order to get nourishment and other necessities of life, while the other grants requests and gives him or her tasks to perform. For in this sense, strictly speaking, someone who lives in servitude should by no means be called a slave but rather an "attendant" or "servant," what the Greeks call *misthotos*. But instead we see that slavery, as defined by jurists, is a status in which someone is unwillingly subjected to the authority of another. And for this reason the name slave or chattel must be assigned. We see this distinction perfectly, to my judgment, in the extant *Sententiae* of Lucius Annaeus Seneca and Publilius Syrus: "If you obey unwillingly, you are a slave; if willingly, you are a servant."[128]

Therefore the question is precisely this: whether Christians are permitted, in keeping with evangelic freedom, to possess other human beings in the manner of personal goods? And, if these human beings properly profess Christianity, should they continue to be subjected to bodily slavery? In order to discuss this, we shall divide all the material that must be covered into two chapters. The first will explore the ancient origins of slavery and will show that its use is accepted among almost all tribes. The second will prove that slavery is not at odds with Christianity.

CHAPTER TWO,

which explores the ancient origin of slavery and shows that nearly all societies made use of it

(1) The most learned people propose that, without a shadow of doubt, every human being is under his own authority according to natural law, and that the common condition of early humankind permitted equal freedom to all humans. It is because we are all similar by origin. There is the same reasoning for the same things, and where there is the same reasoning, there is the same law. The thorny argument of Aristotle, *Politics* 1.5 [1259a38–1260b26], where he judges that in the natural state the difference among people must be recognized, that while one person is free by nature, another may be born a slave, plainly exhibits either humor in a serious context or the arrogance of the Peripatetic school in matters such as this.[129]

(2) The remaining gentiles have discredited this view of Aristotle, though their opinions differed in examining the early origins of slavery, and so they have come close to the enlightening face of truth. No doubt they thought that the rise of slavery was caused by injustice or by chance or by the law of nations. Lucius Annaeus Seneca said that the Roman ranks of knight, freedman and slave were born out of ambition or injustice (*Letters* 31.11).[130] Bisetus, the com-

mentator on Aristophanes, writes the following concerning the comedy *Plutus* ("Wealth"), v. 7, where the groaning slave says to Carius that the condition of slavery was introduced by a spirit:[131]

> "The spirit": Fortune, certainly not nature; but the law of the nations and fortune make persons slaves to others. And, as Harmenopoulos says in his definition of bondage, slavery is a strange custom of the law of nations, out of which arises authority of one over another, something which is opposed to natural law.[132] For nature has made all people free.

This is fortune, which the heathen convinced themselves rules over human affairs arbitrarily, as Horace says in *Odes* 1.34.14–16:[133]

> Greedy fortune takes pleasure in snatching the crown
> from one, amid loud noise,
> and giving it to another.

Indeed it is not nature but human law and accident which have made humans into slaves. This, in fact, is how Harmenopoulos defined slavery.[134]

(3) These passages show us that the origins of slavery do not reach that far back, though its use was certainly taken up and spread, and therefore social distinction between humans should be derived from that source; so I think we should ask when such a change in human relations took place, and where it emanated. To be brief, let us dismiss the

conjectures of certain scholars and throw in our lot with those who believe that slavery arose soon after the flood. After all, the prophet Moses, covering the beginning of the world in a short summary, recounts this in Genesis 9:25. Here it is said that, because Ham mocked his father's nudity, the descendants of Ham, who had this miserable condition imposed on him before his brothers, would bear the mark of perpetual punishment, so that he would be a "slave of slaves to his brothers" (*eved avadim l'echayu*). Alcimus Avitus, bishop of Vienne, described by our forebears as the most elegant writer of sacred literature, writes of the flood, describing it thus in book 4.404–415 of his epic:[135]

> Nature had not yet caused slaves to be so called,
> nor had rank arisen to distinguish masters from servants.
> Among his sons, he who chanced to laugh when he found
> his father Noah naked, a pitiful sight,
> laughed as he rose, already baser,
> defiled and wretchedly stripped.
> When saintly Noah realized it,
> he gave his son to his brothers,
> and the yoke was invented.
> For we are all born from one seed.
> The guilty one is seen to have originated slavery,
> and the free sinner may become a slave through his crime.

(4) That being the case, it is equally clear that this was the moment when slavery entered the earth. And so as mankind was verging on degeneracy more and more every day, it not only grew in strength but was accepted and spread among most peoples, if not all. Those who were

bought at a price, or those who were born to servants, whom they called *vernae*, or those who were captured in war, were compelled into slavery by a certain unspoken consensus, which the law of nations had confirmed. Saint Peter addresses the topic of war-captives with unquestionable authority when he says that *people are slaves to whatever masters them* (II Peter 2:19). The Scholiast to Aristophanes, adding more in a passage already mentioned, is of the same opinion: "Enemy cunning invented slavery, for the law or right of war demands that the defeated become the possession of the victors." For this reason the Greeks seem to have added the term *hoi douloi* to the terms by which slaves are known, as listed by Athenaeus, book 6 page 267b–c—a term which, as Ammonius observes, means "subjected by means of violence," so that captives could not be considered anything other than personal property.[136]

(5) With this law of nations established by popular vote, the use of slavery even became known among the Jews by the divine institution and mandate found in Leviticus 25.[137] More than other peoples, you would find the Romans abounding in slaves, whose various levels and occupations were recorded by jurists. These things, which I shall pass over, are described by Laurentius Pignorius.[138] The slaves of the Jews were either Israelites or Canaanites. There is no need to discuss the Israelites now, as it is abundantly clear from the passage cited that they were not so much slaves as hired servants, and should therefore be so designated.

Nonetheless, anyone who wants to learn how these people, having become impoverished, were once forced to submit to a semblance of slavery, should consult the great writers who make England famous for its literature, and especially John Selden's *De jure naturali et gentium* book 6.7.[139] In truth, those of the Canaanites and other surrounding peoples who descended into slavery were called in a most particular sense, by Hebrew idiom, "slaves" (*avadim*), or rather "those subjected to bankruptcy," for the root of the word has this meaning in Hebrew (*avad*). Nothing can be more cogently concluded, as has been pointed out by Schultens, that immortal beacon of Hebraic studies in our age, in his *Commentary on Job* 1:3, p. 6.[140]

(6) Perhaps the Jews themselves detected something harsh in this term, which is distinguished from "hireling" (*sakir*): this is what Jewish scholars called themselves and their people with the passage of time, so that they might be respected (though captured by enemies and having sunken to a dire state among humans), for they had become useful to the state according to the difference of custom or of place. On the other hand they had once applied the term "slavery" solely to their own slaves. As the aforementioned Selden writes in his *De jure naturali et gentium*, book 19, p. 814: "In no way can it [i.e. the institution of slavery] be destroyed by any simple formula, whether it consists of words, actions, or manumitting by petition."

(7) As Leviticus 25:45–46 adds, it was up to the Jews whether they wished to keep their slaves (*avadim*) in ongoing servitude, by which slaves would continue to be subjected to their masters' descendants and be assigned to all kinds of servile labor, if only any master take care that, incensed with anger, he does not break the limbs of a slave or maidservant with a cruel flogging. When this happened, according to Exodus 21:26–27, slave and maidservant were to be set free by a decision of the court, even against the master's wishes.[141]

(8) Thus the early origins of slavery have been briefly discussed and presented to the studious reader, and the fountain from which it flowed into the rest of the world has been located. At last we reach that point on which the entire axis of our theme turns, so that we can demonstrate that slavery is not contrary to evangelic freedom.

CHAPTER THREE,
which proves that slavery and Christianity are not antithetical

(1) It is clear beyond doubt that most Netherlanders wish to persuade themselves and others in the exchange of debate that Christian freedom can in no way walk in step with slavery in the proper sense. For now in our time it is thought that worship of God must necessarily be cultivated not only with a pure mind, which does not allow itself under the devil's control to be reduced from the spiritual basis that gives it life, but indeed also with a free body. If this opinion, as I would label it, is not on the right lines, at least it can be linked somehow to the views and sayings of fanatics, by which they, charged up with meaningless spirit and arguing that every magistrate in the Christian world should be removed, were unable to proclaim that slavery does not contradict Christianity. This incorrect view would never have occupied the minds of our adversaries had they not formed preposterous ideas of all sorts about the nature of the New Covenant, and were they not ignorant of the ways of the early Christians, or of their own regions, of ancient law and of the more signficant customs.

(2) Concerning the nature of the New Covenant they believe that this freedom promised to believers is just as much corporeal as spiritual. And so, as the Old Covenant

was transformed into the New, slavery which flourished under the Old (as we saw above), now in our age would be thrown out together with the other repealed practices of Mosaic law. All of this is affirmed, they allege, by the witness of II Corinthians 3:17; Galatians 5:1; I Corinthians 7:23 and John 8:32, among other sacred writings.[142]

(3) They think that support and corroboration for their opinion derives from the custom of their regions: on the grounds that slavery is unknown in the Netherlands, since it is forbidden for any person to be cast into slavery, nay more, that every slave who is brought to live here in the Netherlands from some other place is granted bodily freedom as if by tacit consent, and even more if he formally embraces Christianity, so much so that he can no longer be sold by his master at will.

(4) Although these reasons may seem specious to some, still after being called back to a just weighing with a balanced scale, they will easily be found to lack in weight. For my part, I freely assert that the New Covenant gives freedom to people who, through the special grace of the Most High God, are or become participants in it. But how should it be understood? As spiritual and bodily simultaneously? Decidedly not. It is only the spiritual which shakes off from Christian shoulders the burden of ceremonial law which according to Paul and Peter, the fathers were not able to bear, and liberates them so they may undergo the mild yoke of Christ.[143]

(5) The situation should be understood in no other way than this: firstly, innumerable passages in the New Testament itself (of these it will suffice to mention two, Ephesians 6:5 and I Timothy 6:1),[144] and, secondly, those same references made in paragraph 2 above, out of which our opponents construct their case against us, shout this out, and brilliantly throw back the quivering spear at them. No wise person will allege that I will have exceeded the limits of this dissertation if I were to bring this to your attention by means of a rather short listing of the passages cited.

(6) As indeed at II Corinthians 3:17, *where the spirit of the lord is, there is freedom*, it is very clear from the connection between this passage and preceding ones, particularly the sixth, seventh, and thirteenth verses, that freedom as it is mentioned here is opposed by the yoke of slavery in the form of Mosaic law, by which a great number of the Israelites, weighed down by countless ritual observances, multiplied their guilt daily by transgressing the law. And according to the axiom of our unerring teacher in heaven, *everyone who commits sin is a slave to sin* (John 8:34: this passage needs to be discussed more fully below). There is twofold evidence of this slavery. One is that, after committing the idolatry of the golden calf, the Israelites were afraid to approach Moses when he was about to deliver God's commandments to them, his face aglow with divine light, for they thought themselves unworthy to behold the shining

glory of God himself. The other instance is Hebrews 2:15 (on which you should consult Gregory Raphelengius), where Paul seemed to speak about most of the Israelites when he said that *all their lives [they] were held in slavery by the fear of death*.[145] For this well-known saying rings very true:

> Since each mind is aware of its own affairs,
> it conceives hope and fear inside its breast for its own deeds.[146]

Moreover, unless they maintained as much obedience as the law of Moses demands, they were subject to the most dire curse.

FRANCISCUS RAPHELENGIUS
HEBRÆARUM LITERARUM PROFES.

*Franciscus Raphelengius
(1539–1597), professor of Hebrew.
From Johannes van Meurs,
Athenae Batavae (Leiden, 1625).
Leiden University Library*

How much the law of commission would have been granted to all Moses' successors as a result of this sin of *moscholatreia* ("calf-worship"), by which the Israelites transgressed God's law, just as Adam had done;[147] how much can be extrapolated from it, seeing that the scribes and pharisees burdened the shoulders of humankind with loads that were heavy and hard to carry, though they themselves did not even lift a finger to move them. The apostle Paul shows that this most powerful and widespread reign of prescribed law, and the servile fear of the Israelites, came to an end, with the New Dispensation superseding the Old. Just as for the truly faithful, however many were led by Christ to remove the fog and extract the inner meaning of the law, sin would no longer have dominion over them through the precepts of that law, as we read in Romans 6:14.[148] On the other hand, since they were rewarded with the freedom of the glory of God's children, a brightly shining sign [of the New Dispensation] is described in this chapter, a sign by which, even in this mortal life, God's glory is offered to be looked at in their uncovered faces as if in a mirror. And so the main argument returns to this: along with our most distinguished leader and any other names that might be more celebrated, if that were possible, we maintain that in this case Paul distinguishes the literal sense in Mosaic law, under the name of the letter (*to gramma*), from its mystical sense which he calls the spirit (*to pneuma*), something that was not understood in its full sense until the time of the Gospel.[149] From this it follows that in this entire chapter we should not debate physical freedom for even one syllable, but rather we should confine ourselves only to spiritual freedom, freedom that is drawn from the fundamentals of Christian freedom.

(7) Galatians 5:1 refers to, in fact demands, that very spiritual freedom which I have just mentioned: *For freedom Christ has set us free; stand fast therefore, and do not submit*

again to a yoke of slavery. For Paul, the most reliable interpreter of sacred texts, speaks at Galatians 4:22 about the
two sons of Abraham, and of how slavery followed the one
born to a slave woman, whereas freedom followed the one
born to a free woman. At verse 24 he says that this is an
allegory, by which expression he takes pains to indicate
that in the following discussion he will propose that slavery
is the outer observance of Mosaic law, called the covenant
of Sinai, and that by freedom he means the Dispensation of
the New Testament, freed from all those rituals. This distinction, as they well realize, encourages the Galatians not
to submit to the yoke of Sinai at the hands of the Judaizers,
who insisted on emphasizing the need for circumcision.

(8) The third example, from the first letter to the Corinthians, 7:23: *You were bought with a price; do not become
slaves of men,* will not be so easily answered. Nonetheless, if
examined diligently under its own internal light and
viewed from all angles, these words of Paul will, in their
context, fight all the more clearly for our cause rather than
for that of our adversaries. For nobody can fail to see that it
is shown here that it was contested among the Corinthians
whether slavery in the ordinary sense could coexist with
Christian freedom: and so in those times the very same subject which we are now discussing was being investigated.
This question, which was being discussed by greater minds
than ours, as was right, the Corinthians handed over in a
letter to be decided by Paul, together with other questions.

But he would reply (v. 20) that he wanted the general rule to be observed that religious doctrine by no means removes differences of status.[150] Paul concludes from this (v. 21) that any slave who should give his name to Christ should be content with that condition: likewise if he could become free by honorable means, that is, not against God's will, he would prefer freedom over slavery. He goes on to declare (v. 22) that external or personal freedom is not essential to the worship of God. A remarkable paradox indicates this fact: whoever has been called a slave in the Lord becomes a freedman of the Lord and, conversely, whoever has been called free becomes Christ's slave. From this he concludes, in our passage, that everyone whether slave or free should recognize that he has been bought with the precious blood of Christ. That person must therefore make sure not to subject himself willingly to servile status among gentiles, in accordance with the repulsive custom of that age whereby many hired themselves out to trainers and masters in order to fight against beasts and gladiators, as indeed the renowned Claudius Salmasius, that untiring student of ancient literature, said in his response to Milton, p. 20.[151]

Since this is the case it becomes easy to see that here too our adversaries will find no defense for their opinion. Moreover, Paul's response to the Corinthians carries so much evidential weight that he forestalls our adversaries at every turn and they can no longer challenge us. They claim that slavery was tolerated for a long time in the age of the apostles until, with the light of the Gospel growing brighter each day and the Christian community establishing a firmer, safer base, slavery was completely stopped among Christians. If this were to be established, who does not see, I ask, that the apostle Paul would have had to discuss the duration of slavery when he discussed the subject at such a suitable point? But though he says nothing about the matter, we can see clearly enough that our view is strengthened, as it were, by new fortifications.

(9) Finally, let us add John 8:32: *And you will know the truth, and the truth will make you free.* These words of our Savior to the Jews seem at first glance to offer the greatest shelter of a contrary view. This is particularly so if it is borne in mind that the word *eleutheroun* ("to set free"), as has been long established by those best versed in Greek, was commonly used by the greatest Greek writers to signify manumission, with which people become free or freedmen. Above all, it can be seen in Euripides' *Heracleidae*, where a certain mistress is moved to promise freedom to her servant with these words (l. 788–89):[152]

> Dearest man, this day has taken you
> to freedom, because of this message.

Hence the term "slave" (*doulos*) is opposed to "free" (*eleutheros*) in a dialogue of Aeschines Socraticus.[153] Our adversaries take encouragement from the thought that it can be concluded from the responses which the Jews gave to Christ's saying, that by freedom Christ had in mind not spiritual but rather physical freedom. To be sure, the Jews responded indignantly to Christ (John 8:33): *We are descendants of Abraham, and have never been in bondage to anyone. How is it that you say, "You will be made free"?* John Selden once conjectured about this very passage in his exegesis, book 6.9:

> Surely they are merely saying here, on the strength of their traditional teaching, that they never suffered *inner* slavery; nowhere do they deny the other, *outer*, kind (to use a distinction we have made above in the case of the Jews) of a people either captured or given into slavery.

(10) But nobody who pursues the truth can ignore the fact that each person is the best interpreter of his or her own words. The following passage leaves us in no doubt that the Jews misinterpreted Christ's intentions either out of malicious fabrication or out of ignorance (as with Nicodemus who understood rebirth in the bodily sense), while their innermost senses were bent more on carnal than on spiritual affairs at that time. Christ makes absolutely clear what he wished to signify by liberty, that is liberty from the sin by which the devil rules all those who have not yet fled to Christ the savior through his health-giving faith. In this way the person who has been devoted to sin, that is to pleasure and desire, is called a slave of sin par excellence. This is proven not only by much testimony of the scriptures but also by the agreement between the Greek fathers, as we call them, and the gentiles themselves; likewise, in copious

fashion, J. Caspar Suicerus in the first volume of his *Thesaurus of the church*, under the word "slavery," number 2, p. 956.[154] Moreover Joachim Kühn should be consulted in his *Annotations to Aelian's variae historiae*, book 2.4, p. 94.[155]

(11) And so we distinguish between slavery of conscience or sin and civil slavery; between heavenly law and the law of the courtroom; between freedom of the spirit and freedom of the body. Christ talks about heavenly law and about slavery of conscience or the spirit, from which we are defended by the New Covenant, as Johannes Crocius has pointed out well on page 181 with reference to the first epistle to Timothy 6.1, the first instance in the teaching of a distinction of status.[156] Henry More of Cambridge discusses what freedom under the New Covenant involves, in his *Opera theologica*, book 9.7, pp. 393–94, paras. 8–10:[157]

(1) The faithful are freed from the fussy and excessive encumbrances of ritual observance, so that we are no longer caught up in the toils of silly superstition and its practices, things which are of such a nature that they cannot show the way to everlasting life or extend Christ's kingdom on earth.

(2) The faithful are freed from their sins, that is from pride, envy, hatred, anger, grief, avarice, and every desire, so that this freedom can lead us to justice, which cannot fail to presuppose the effective persuasion of truth. Therefore it seems that I was not wrong to conjecture that Christ, our heavenly teacher, meant with the phrase, *The*

truth will make you free (John 8:32) that believers would be sanctified through truth in the word of God, as John says (17:17).[158] Anyone who wishes to learn more fully about the nature and aspects of Christian freedom should look at John Calvin's *Institutes* (3.19).

(12) But if anyone does not agree with these solutions, let them read the brief letter of Paul to Philemon, and they will recognize with me that "where there is evidence there is no need for words."[159] From this letter it is more clearly elucidated than the light of noon that a slave named Onesimus who secretly fled from his master Philemon to Rome was there initiated by Paul into the rudiments of Christian doctrine, and afterwards sent back to his master. As one can infer from the context of the letter, Philemon is beseeched humanely through prayers to take Onesimus back without flogging him, not in terms of his rights but out of brotherly love, on account of the shared faith which will make Onesimus more fit than before to perform his future duties.

From these things it is abundantly clear, as we wished, that the nature of the New Covenant demands only *spiritual* freedom in order that we can worship God, not necessarily *external* freedom. As a result, differences of status in Christianity by no means have to be removed. The illustrious Hugo Grotius, whose name continues to shine like a star in the scholarly universe, even after his death, has some comments well worth reading in the last part of the fifteenth verse of his letter.[160] See also Paul Voet's *Institutes* 1.3.4.[161]

(13) If anyone still objects to this demonstration of unquestionable truth which, unless I am completely mistaken, we have deduced from the nature of the Gospel, that person will necessarily face extreme and intractable difficulties. For it is clear even to catechumens that the Gospel very often presents the spiritual kingdom of God (to borrow a phrase from the kingdoms, kings, and lords of this world) in such a way that Christ Jesus, the one and most loyal shepherd of our souls, is presented as the most glorious king and lord of that kingdom—Christ, who having suffered much servitude, gives laws to his subjects, whom he himself gained with his own blood, and who are therefore warned always to recall that they were bought for this price and should glorify God in body and soul. Reference is made here to the right of a master in antiquity over slaves whom he had bought for personal use.

How can we explain and understand these and similar phenomena if it is held—so runs the argument of our adversaries—that the name and use of slavery considered in and of itself seem so inimical to the nature of the New Covenant that Christians are not allowed to keep a Christian slave? Is it, I ask, that all these phrases have been taken from a source which is forbidden to Christians? Moreover, I ask, to what deceit and injustice would the door be opened? For all people, and consequently also slaves, can easily feign Christ's name. They would do this more readily if the reward of such a wrongdoing were freedom. It would happen in such a way that masters, being frequently tricked by this ruse, would be denied what is rightfully theirs, and in such a way that many in their great desire to retain their own property, would cease from their efforts to convert slaves but rather oppose conversion. We all understand that this is far from the wishes of the righteous.

(14) Anyone who lays prejudice aside and gives due attention to these things which we have said from the fourth paragraph of this chapter up to this point will happily agree with me how deceptively the argument was at one time forced upon the Christian world by a tract under the title, *On the manumission of Turkish slaves by baptism*. Christian Thomasius, a man of great talent and distinction, refuted this argument and showed in chapter 8 of his *Various questions of history, philosophy and law* how false it was when exposed.[162]

(15) But finally, in order that I might back off from this demonstration of my own beliefs derived from the nature of the New Covenant, let me conclude with the words of John Calvin, that man of austere holiness, that man famous among those who were the first to spread the true Gospel in his own time, who publicly refuted the opinion of our adversaries when he said:[163]

*John Calvin, theologian (1509–1564).
With permission of Calvin College,
Grand Rapids, Michigan*

The person who knows how to discern the difference between body and soul, between this present, transient life and that eternal life to come, will have no difficulty in understanding that Christ's spiritual kingdom and the civil order are entirely different matters. Therefore it is vanity on the part of the Jews to seek and enclose Christ's kingdom within the parts of this world. Let us rather ponder what scripture clearly teaches, namely that the fruit which we pluck through God's benefaction is spiritual; and we will remember to keep within its own limits all that freedom which is promised and given to us in him. For why is it that the same apostle Paul who bids us to be firm and not to submit to the *yoke of slavery* [Galatians 5:1] elsewhere forbids slaves to be anxious about their status [I Corinthians 7:21], if it were not that spiritual freedom can perfectly well coexist with civil bondage? It is in this light that such statements should be understood, that in God's kingdom there is neither Jew nor Greek, neither male nor female, neither slave nor free [Galatians 3:28]. By the same token, there is neither Jew nor Greek, neither circumcised nor uncircumcised, neither barbarian nor Scythian, neither slave nor free. But Christ is all and in all [Colossians 3:11]. By this is meant that it makes no difference what one's status among humans is or under what nation's laws one lives, since Christ's kingdom does not consist in these things at all.

(16) Now that the first rank of our enemies has been crushed, I am glad to say, let us attack the second. These contend that acceptance of our thesis is an unwise withdrawal from the ancient and accepted practice of the early Christians, among whom the manumission of slaves was celebrated as a mark of exceptional piety. This is particularly the case at Easter, when they went in memory of the glorious resurrection of our savior, as we read in Gregory of Nyssa, who flourished around A.D. 370: "On this day the bonds are removed, the debtor released, the slave freed by a beneficent and humane proclamation and edict of the church."[164]

Our opponents think we must concede from this that the early Christians understood, and in fact proved, that personal bondage and Christian freedom are mutually contradictory. And so, in order to respond to this argument as briefly as possible, I would prefer the issue at hand to be considered on a firm basis of law rather than practice, for in this way we are not inquiring into what the ancient Christians actually did as a result of their exceptional and always praiseworthy goodwill and clemency, but rather into what needed to be done on account of Christian freedom, and into what it is incumbent upon all Christians to observe diligently at all times. While our opponents relate the manumission of slaves to the last of these, it will scarcely be evident by which person, at what time, and on which occasion this kind of manumission was instituted among Christians; and it will tie them into such a knot that the absurdity of their argument will become clear when compared with our thesis.

(17) Writers of church history allege that Constantine the Great originated the custom of manumitting slaves in the church.[165] As Sozomen writes (1.9):[166]

> It seems worthwhile, as I begin this discussion, to list here the laws made for the use of those who were given freedom in the church. Partly in order to maintain a careful observation of the laws, and partly for the sake of owners who unwillingly released them, since it would be very difficult for anyone to acquire greater freedom than being given Roman citizenship, he passed three laws decreeing that all who had been given their freedom in the church, with priests as witnesses, would be granted Roman citizenship. Sufficiently clear indications of this holy institution survive even into our age. Indeed the custom is maintained to this day, that consecrated laws concerning this matter are first written down in the records of manumissions. These laws were promulgated by Constantine, who devoted all his care and thought to reinforcing Christianity.

Relating to this topic, the following can be read in Nicephorus Callistus (7.46):[167]

> Constantine also granted freedom to the church by legislation, and after having been given freedom, witnessed by priests, they would be enrolled among the number of Roman citizens. The passage of time confirms these things

since this custom has been approved and has prevailed over many years up to the present time. He established laws of this sort with great zeal, and with them he industriously spread the worship of God.

With this, finally, the "tripartite" *Ecclesiastical history*, as it is known, concurs (1.9):

Because of the subtlety of the laws, owners unintentionally suffered difficulty in bestowing the greater freedom which they call Roman citizenship. Therefore Constantine passed three laws, decreeing that through this pious measure all who had been freed in the church, witnessed by priests, would enjoy Roman citizenship, and the present time still preserves signs of this measure. For it was customary for written laws concerning freedom to be given priority in manumissions. Therefore Constantine took this step, clearly eager to honor religion in every respect.

This is confirmed by the first and second laws in the *Book of those who have been manumitted in the church*. For the first law is as follows:

It was resolved long ago that people would be more likely to grant their slaves freedom of the Lord in the Catholic church if they could do so in the presence of the people and with Christian priests assisting. In order to preserve the memory of the event, records would be set down in the manner of public proceedings which they themselves would sign as witnesses. Therefore, with justification can freedom be given or bequeathed by each of you however you wish, as long as there is evidence of your intention.

119

The second law runs as follows:

> Those who, out of religious reasons and within the embrace of the church, grant freedom to their deserving slaves should do so under that law by which Roman citizenship is usually conferred in a completely performed ceremony. But with the following reservation that this law may be relaxed for those who grant it in the presence of priests. (And so forth.)

It is true that the words of the first law, "It was resolved long ago," seem to disagree with the authors quoted above, so much so that we should not consider Constantine to be the first proponent of manumission in the church. But I see that for two reasons discrepancy and ambiguity are eliminated by the most eminent experts in the law-court who have focused their minds on these words. For they observe that before Constantine passed the recorded laws, upon being consulted, he either responded with a letter that it was permitted to do so, or he himself passed the three laws concerning this issue, as we heard from Sozomen a little earlier. From this they conclude that the first of these laws fell into disuse with the passage of time. But however these things came about, I do know this much: it is most explicitly established that nobody records this law and custom before Constantine's conversion from paganism to the purer religion, but that this type of manumission certainly grew stronger among Christians between A.D. 312 and 316. Since this is so, as my prerogative I ask the opponents why this custom was eventually introduced after so long a stretch of time since the age of the Apostles and the first Christians, who were not in any doubt that piety was strongly linked to charity? Had that age not tasted the sweet fruit of benevolent Christian freedom? Or were slaves of that period outside the bosom of the church? If anyone thinks either of these to be the case, they not only display their own ignorance but they also make futile attacks on the most evident truths which we have already proven.

(18) Concerning the point at which Constantine ordered slaves to be manumitted in the church, anyone who ponders carefully the writers cited will understand that this kind of manumission had been recommended to church authorities not so much to preserve Christian freedom as to increase their authority even in human affairs. For now those who had victimized the Christians had been either restrained or killed, and the church was in a better position and it seemed that wonderful peace reigned everywhere; the praised emperor decreed, on the strength of his affection for and reverence toward those who professed the religion, that the law of manumission would be in the power of the bishops, for humanity persuaded all people, and particularly Christians, whom it behooved to be more compassionate than the gentiles; indeed greater trust was put in them than in secular judges for reliable and persuasive judgments. For Constantine had sensed that, to use the words of Sozomen, "In the careful observation of the laws considerable difficulty attends the acquisition of the greater

freedom [i.e. of citizenship]." For certainly during the census which preceded the method of manumission within the church, and which the foremost jurists believe should be specified in the Second Law as "performed ritual observance," it was custom at Rome that slaves would gain their freedom if they were registered by their masters in the census of Roman citizens.

(19) These laws of Constantine on no account obligated individual Christians to free all of their slaves, Gentile or Christian, whether they so wished or not, as if slavery had been finally discovered to be at loggerheads with Christian freedom; but instead they concern only those who are well-deserving enough to be granted freedom selectively. The ancients once treated their faithful slaves in the same way, according to Terence, *Andria*, act 1, scene 1 [lines 37–38]:[168]

> My slave, I made you become my freedman
> because you have served me so freely.

The words of Saint Augustine urge us to believe it (*Sermon* 21.6):[169]

> You take your slaves to the church to be manumitted. Quiet reigns. Your petition is read aloud, or your wish is made known. You say that you are manumitting your slave, because he has served you faithfully in every way.

(20) I emphasize this all the more strongly. In the very superstitious age of Marculfus the Monk, who, according to Bignon's notes in his first book of *Laws*, flourished around

A.D. 660 in France, it was thought that Constantine was the originator of manumission in the church, and it was entirely up to masters to decide on the kind of freedom granted to the slaves whom they were manumitting. In fact Marculfus cites the following in his *Laws*, book 2.33:

> N. N. to his beloved male or female slave: Because of the loyalty and service with which you have served me as a household slave, and for the remission of my sins, I absolve you from every bond of slavery, on condition that you continue to serve me while I live, whereas if you outlive me, may you be free. (And so it continues.)

It must be added that the purchase of slaves was practiced during that age, as is clear from Bignon's *Formulae*, which should evidently be ascribed to Marculfus. For we read in the second chapter:

> In the name of God, I am selling N. N. to this buyer, my brother, a splendid lord. I have decided, not by supposed right, nor under duress, but by the proper decision of my own will, to sell you this homeborn slave from today henceforth in terms of my rights. (And so it goes on.)

Since this is the case, it becomes brilliantly clear how false it is that the manumission of slaves in the church was introduced entirely to eradicate slavery from the whole Christian world on account of Christian freedom and so that good doctrines could be spread everywhere—so much so that all Christians, even in our own time, would be obliged to preserve this custom.

(21) But perhaps the poet was correct to predict that "even to those already conquered, valor returns to the heart" (Virgil, *Aeneid* 2.376).[170] Opponents will rise against us and say, "Though we agree with the foregoing proof, we nonetheless uphold, on the strength of the passage from Marculfus, that several early Christians thought it a sign of worth as well as of conscientiousness if someone released a male or female slave, and we should always strive for what appears to have pleased God in the past." Certainly we do not deny that many Christians of antiquity, particularly the Franks, were brought round to this opinion by certain people of the church who inherited the law of manumission instituted by Constantine. But I do not at all hesitate to call it silly and superstitious. For because there is no reference among the aforementioned ecclesiastical historians to this view, derived from those *Laws* by which slaves were freed in the age of Marculfus, and because such a view is so far from the divine truth, let those who have received higher faculties from God and who have been taught by our heavenly teacher discern that we are not allowed to abandon God's serious teachings, his judgment, his mercy, and faith, so that we can adhere to human customs. To make this clear to our adversaries I shall simply include three passages from Marculfus himself. But please restrain your laughter, my friends! At book 2.32 we read:

> Whoever releases a rightful bond of servitude can be sure that the Lord will repay him in the future. And so in God's name, in order to save our souls and for eternal reward, my

wife and I release you from all bonds of slavery in our household from this day onward.

Likewise we read at 2.34:

If we release any of our slaves from the shackles of slavery, we ensure that we shall receive recompense in the future. Therefore in God's name and for eternal reward, I free you from all chains of servitude so that you may lead a free life from this day onward, just as if you had been born to free parents, and you may not give your service to any of my heirs and descendants or to anyone else, unless with a complete guarantee of freedom you should hold yourself to whomever of my heirs you should choose, and once I have passed away you should perform a mass and light a candle for me at each anniversary. (And so on.)

Finally, in his appendix (chapter 13), the following stands out:

As long as almighty God allows us to have a healthy body in this life, we ought to think frequently about the health of our souls so that we deserve to have our sins reduced a little. And so in God's name, I have by my rights released this slave as a free person, in order to cure my soul and diminish my sins, and so that in the future God may see fit to show forgiveness to me. (And what follows.)

(22) But, so as not to be more long-winded than I intended, let me proceed to show that those people, however many they are, who try to prove to themselves and to others that slavery in the strictest sense no longer prevails in

the Netherlands, claiming that both laws and Christian principles oppose it, are doing so more out of ignorance than from any solid basis. Since any citizen or resident alien can relish complete freedom here, according to the privileges granted by the counts and kings of these regions, nobody who has any knowledge of Dutch affairs can deny that this must be attributed to political considerations. For, both before and after the Netherlands was enlightened by the health-giving glow of the Reformation, slavery was a well-known phenomenon here, as is testified not only by jurists of former times but also by the more recent ones who have mentioned the provinces of the Netherlands in their work.

(23) Indeed, the most distinguished jurist Peter Gudelinus writes as follows in his *Commentaries on the New Law, book 1, ch. 4, On aspects of the New Law which concern the condition of slaves, p. 56*:[171]

At one time among Christians here, just as elsewhere, the treatment of purchased and home-born slaves was extremely harsh, and even the church kept slaves, as the records show, until the gradual rise of Christian charity induced many to manumit their slaves. Finally, there were hardly any slaves anywhere, as Johann Molanus noted in *Canons* book 3.[172] It is not known when exactly this came about. Around A.D. 1200 there were still slaves in Italy and Germany, as the papal records indicate in the decrees under the titles, *Slaves should not be ordained* and *On the marriage of slaves*. In the same book mentioned above, Molanus adds that the Church of Saint Peter in Leuven possesses the document of the manumission of a certain person which took place in that church in A.D. 1250. Therefore it is probably only for three hundred years, or a little more, that the possession of slaves began to be abolished in the Netherlands and in most other places. But the use and sale of slaves are still retained to this very day in Portugal, in other parts of Spain, and in some jurisdictions which border the Turks—there it is customary for slaves to retain their status though they renounce Islam and are taught Christianity. This should not seem absurd, since it has been shown that the enslavement of people and the power of a master do not contradict divine law.

So that no influential person of contrary opinion can imagine that the weapons to be used against us lie buried beneath these words, "until the gradual rise of Christian charity induced many to manumit their slaves, and finally there were hardly any slaves anywhere," I shall take away from that person every opportunity of recovering his strength. We readily concede that Christian charity does not permit Christians to brutalize their slaves and it offers, with the passage of time, the opportunity for slavery to be utterly removed. In this way it has always been permitted for any Christian to manumit his slave, should he so wish. But we deny that this proceeds from any specific instruction in the Gospel.

Paul Christanaeus may be added to Gudelinus, and in his *Decisions of the Dutch senate* vol. 4.80.2–3 nearly the same words are found.[173] Ulrich Huber, who dates the abolition of

HUGO GROTIUS.IC.

*Hugo Grotius, jurist
(1583–1645). From Meurs,
Athenae Batavae.
Leiden University Library*

slavery among Christians to the later period, said this in the foreword to his *Institutes on personal law*: "From this time, about A.D. 1212 or thereabouts, Christians ceased to sell each other into slavery."[174] And Hugo Grotius in his *Introduction to the law of Holland, written in Dutch,* says that the use of slaves in the Netherlands was not stopped until three hundred years ago.

(24) Should anyone ask for what reason the name and practice of slavery has ended within the Netherlands, I would want them to hear what Paul Voet has to say in his *Institutes* 1.3.4:

> Since the provinces of the Netherlands Federation are opposed to the law of slavery, having achieved their freedom by law and by arms, any slaves who might come over to us from elsewhere or enter the boundaries of our territory should by the very fact of their coming here obtain their freedom. In order that they might be all the more located in the Netherlands Federation as a safe haven, those people who have arrived in our jurisdiction and come to our guardianship and protection should not be exposed to those things from which they have fled.

From all of this the following is more than clear enough to anyone: every slave who is brought here from elsewhere enjoys complete freedom in the Netherlands, not so much as a result of the laws and principles of the Gospel but rather due to political reasons.[175]

(25) What a firm basis does our conclusion rest upon. On the strength of this, granting the opinion of our adversaries concerning the state of the Netherlands, it is necessary to show how, even when Christian freedom is intact, there remain not only certain traces of earlier slavery but also, more importantly, the buying and selling of slaves. This is the case in many other Christian states in which all people profess Christianity, albeit with different opinions and in different ways. Paul Voet, in the passage mentioned above, confirms this, as do the battery of our other key witnesses.

> Nevertheless, certain traces of ancient slavery have remained in Germany, Poland, Muscovy, Transylvania, Prussia, and even in the Zutphen and Arnhem Quarters of Gelderland.[176]

And a little later:

> In the kingdom of England, though harsh slavery has been abolished, some people are attached to the land, others work just like slaves for a period on a contract basis; they are called apprentices.

Concerning the purchase and sale of slaves in the manner of cattle, you see what Jean Bodin has to say in the context of the Portuguese (*De republica* 1.5).[177]

(26) To be sure, the most learned and meritorious persons in the state do not hesitate to wish that personal slavery, which in our time has been partly or completely abolished among most Christians, should be reinstituted, inasmuch as it is extremely useful to the state, but restored in such a way that it is in keeping with Christian clemency, rather than brutality. For it is absolutely certain that countless troubles, such as cannot be enumerated easily, would result from the discontinuation of slavery. The most esteemed Busbecq leans toward this view in his *Turkish Letter* 3, pp. 160–61 (Leiden 1633):[178]

> I do not know whether the person who first abolished slavery did us a favor. If run justly, leniently and according to the precepts of Roman law, public slavery in particular could have remained, and there would have been no need for crucifixion and the gibbet to coerce those who have nothing other than their life and their freedom, and whom poverty forces to commit some kind of crime. Freedom without possessions does not always promote honorable activity. Not everybody's nature can endure resourceless freedom and not everyone is born so that they can have control over themselves and know by their own judgment what is right. They need the leadership and rule of their betters, like a prop; in no other way will they put an end to their misdeeds. By the same token there are certain animals whose fierceness is always to be feared unless constrained by chains. Indeed the weaker mind is ruled by a master's authority, and the master lives by the slave's work. The Turks derive enormous benefit, both public and private,

from slaves: they look after their domestic affairs very effectively by means of slave labor. And so, as the proverb goes, they say that someone who has even a single slave does not seem poor. But if any business must be done, anything carried out, built or demolished in public life, they do it by the assiduous work of slaves. Nowhere can we match the grandeur of ancient monuments. Why is that? We are bereft of manual labor, that is of slave labor. Let me keep silent on the subject of how much the ancients learned from slaves in attaining all types of knowledge.

On the other hand Potgiesserus, relying on the judgments and opinions of great people, especially Busbecq, proves in his *Prolegomena on the status of slaves*, paras. 33–35, in general, not only that humankind reaps greater benefits from slave than from hired labor; but also, in particular, that there would be a massing of dishonest and lazy people who would wander around and consume the food of their fellow-citizens and others, thereby weakening them, an evil that would come about unless slavery continues to proliferate on a large scale among all Christians.[179]

(27) Lest I continue indefinitely, I can, I think, safely draw the following conclusion from the above discussion, even though I by no means concur with every opinion of the most learned writers mentioned above: that slavery in no way contradicts Christian freedom—slavery, which indeed has been repealed here in the Netherlands out of some sense of benevolence and clemency or for political expediency, not because of divine law. From this it follows naturally that slavery does not impede the spread of the

Gospel in those Christian colonies where it prevails right up to the present day. For this reason, a kingdom most amicable and pleasing to God can and should be built for both masters and slaves, educated in the better religious practices. This is what Paul recommends to Philemon (v. 16).[180] And in this way slaves will certainly in the end be as prepared as possible for the will of their masters, as we read in Ephesians 6:5–8: *Slaves, be obedient to those who are your earthly masters, with fear and trembling, in singleness of heart, as to Christ.* On these lines, another passage will grow deep roots in the minds of those masters who have not cast off the character of a Christian gentleman (v. 9): *Masters, do the same to them, and forebear threatening, knowing that he who is both their master and yours is in heaven, and that there is no partiality with him.*

Henry Velse, esteemed pastor of the Church of the Hague and an erudite man if ever there was, has pointed out the ways and means by which this kingdom may be founded and strengthened under good auspices, in the historical preface appended to the *Detailed reports on the founding of Christianity among the heathen on the Coromandel and Malabar coast, written by the Danish missionaries at Tranquebar.*[181] Here that incomparable theologian has reviewed and refuted the doubts of certain people with which they were troubled (paras. 46–47), and discussed in a logical fashion whether the teachings of the Gospel, which will promote and serve this religious work, can be handed down to slaves without ill effect (48–53).

* * * * * *

APPENDIX 1
Two prefaces to Capitein's translation
of religious texts[1]

Translation of the Our Father, of the Twelve Articles of Faith and of the Ten Commandments, into the African language used between Abrowarie and Apam [i.e. Fante]—done in literal fashion by Jacobus Elisa Johannes Capitein, Predikant (chaplain) based at Elmina, published at his own request through the agency of Hieronymus de Wilhem, in Leiden, in 1744, by Jacobus de Beunje.

> At that time I will change the speech of the peoples to a pure speech, that all of them may call on the name of the Lord and serve him with one accord. From beyond the rivers of Ethiopia my suppliants, my scattered ones, shall bring my offering. (Zephaniah 3:9–10)

Preface:
[The translator] to the Christian reader

Behold, dear Christian reader: here is the very first beginning we make toward laying the foundation of Christendom among our African and mulatto schoolchildren at the Castle of the West Indies Company in St. George

---

1. Reprinted as an appendix to H. M. J. Trutenau's edition of *Christian Protten's Introduction to the Fante and Accra (Gã) Languages (1764)* (Afro-Presse/Luzon: London, 1971), 59–60.

133

d'Elmina. Do not by any means believe that this translation, which was undertaken to see whether the entire [Fante] language can be written down, is perfect; but rather that in the course of time it will be refined, so that God will open his door wider to us.

Elmina   Jacobus Elisa Johannes Capitein
3 August 1743   Predikant at Elmina

The publisher to the reader

The Reverend Mr. Capitein was correct to say in his preface that this translation is not perfect: the observant reader will agree with me that certain words in our [Dutch] language cannot be expressed in the African language [of Fante]. As a result, the sense of "eternity" at the end of the Lord's Prayer is omitted; of "eternal life" in the final Article of belief; likewise the concept of "holy" in the third, eighth, and ninth of the same Articles; and "holy" at the end of the fourth Commandment.

From a particular property of the Fante language it is evident that at the beginning of the Lord's Prayer we find the phrase, *Father of us all* [and not *Our Father*]. And we can surmise, from the fact that in the tenth Commandment a horse is mentioned instead of an ass, that the long-eared animal [i.e. ass] is not to be found in the translator's native country.

In particular, I must warn the reader about a difficulty that comes up in the fourth Commandment. The phrase we have put between brackets, (*nor your servant*), is not to be found in the [original] Dutch version: it is clear that a word with this sense is indeed to be found in the [Fante] language, since it is used in the tenth Commandment, where *sússo návra babesía, sússo návra bennîn* is translated as *neither your manservant nor your maidservant*, which appears to be comparable. On the other hand, I can find no words in the Fante version to correspond to the Dutch phrase, *neither your son nor your daughter*.

At all events, it seems to me that the manuscript sent by the Reverend Capitein to the Directors contains an oversight at this point. Because of the remoteness of the translator's current location, he cannot be consulted about this oversight, and the situation is exacerbated by the fact that the [Fante] language is not known locally here in the Netherlands. However, it is incumbent upon me to give warning to the reader.

APPENDIX 2
African intellectuals in 18th-century Europe

Capitein the scholar and missionary has already been presented in the introduction. In the attempt to provide a wider context for him, there follow here brief biographies of a number of African-born persons who spent some time in Europe during the 18th Century, and may be considered either scholars or missionaries or both. There are difficult questions of definition, when, for example, Frederick Pedersen Svane (no. 5 below) was a missionary of sorts, though not officially sanctioned by the church; and, when, to take another example, Granman Quassie (ca. 1690–ca. 1783) received only enough education to be an interpreter for his Dutch owners in Surinam in dealing with the rebel maroons, and did not come to Europe until late in life, and then only on two brief visits.[1] Furthermore, Francis Williams (no. 3) was not, strictly speaking, African-born,

---

1. For reasons that should be clear, Quassie has not received detailed coverage in this appendix. On him, see Allison Blakely, *Blacks in the Dutch World*, 253–56. Richard Price, "Kwasimukamba's gambit," *Bijdragen tot de Taal-, Land- en Volkekunde* 135 (1979): 151–69, has presented Quassie as an opportunistic double-agent, on the strength of a comparison between local (Saramaka) oral history and British written accounts. As a translator Quassie was fluent in the "Negro-English, Carib and Arawak languages," playing a central role in negotiations between the British and the escaped slaves. He was reputed to possess magical powers; various herbal remedies and potions were named after him, so well was he known in the Dutch world: see the article *quassia* in the *Oxford English Dictionary* (2nd ed., 1989).

but Jamaican-born of African descent.

Nonetheless, what these individuals do have in common is that each was African or else had direct ancestral links with Africa, and each received some schooling or training while in Europe. In some cases they wrote academic works and taught at universities (Juan Latino and Anton Wilhelm Amo, nos. 1 and 4); in other cases they were trained as missionaries and later practiced as such (Svane and Philip Quaque, no. 7); but, with the partial exception of Protten, none of them came close to matching Capitein in combining scholarship with ministry.

The coverage here is, of necessity, highly selective: a fuller array of African visitors to Europe is provided by Hans Werner Debrunner, *Presence and Prestige: Africans in Europe: a history of Africans in Europe before 1918* (Basel: Basler Afrika Bibliographien, 1979). For all these persons, the problematic nature of sources is extreme, when what is "known" about many of them derives mostly from sources composed by writers making a point with regard to the morality of slavery. Debrunner's work is part of a remarkably continuous tradition of scholarship going back to the late 18th century.

The first scholar to write a history of black intellectuals was the Abbé Henri Grégoire (1750–1831), whose treatise was written as an act of opposition to slavery and as a means of winning others for the cause. Grégoire was a member of the philanthropic *Amis des Noirs*, a group which led the antislavery cause in Revolutionary France.[2] The original title of Grégoire's work leaves no doubt about its thrust: *Concerning the literature of the Negroes, or research on their intellectual faculties, their moral qualities, and their writings; followed by accounts of the life and works of Negroes who have distinguished themselves in the sciences, letters, and arts.*[3] Subsequent works, notably Wilson Armistead's 568-page *Tribute for the Negro* (Manchester, 1848), recycle much of Grégoire's content, share its practical thrust of opposing slavery, and have in turn themselves been recycled.[4] Thus the problem is that so many of the older accounts have been in a context of celebration that they hamper the task of analysis.

---

2. On Grégoire, see the introduction by Thomas Cassirer and Jean-François Brière, trs. and eds., *On the Cultural Achievements of Negroes* (Amherst: University of Massachusetts Press, 1996). David Brion Davis, *The Problem of Slavery in the Age of Revolution*, esp. 111, situates him relative to the *Amis*. The standard account of Grégoire's life is Ruth Necheles, *The Abbé Grégoire, 1787–1831: the odyssey of an egalitarian* (Westport, Conn.: Greenwood, 1971).

3. *De la littérature des nègres, ou Recherches sur leurs facultés intellectuelles, leurs qualités morales et leur littérature; suivies de Notices sur la vie et les ouvrages des Nègres qui se sont distingués dans les Sciences, les Lettres et les Arts* (Paris: Maradan, 1808).

4. Tellingly, Armistead's full title reads: *A tribute for the Negro; being a vindication of the moral, intellectual, and religious capabilities of the coloured portion of mankind; with particular reference to the African race* (Manchester: Irwin, 1848). For the substantial afterlife of Armistead, two examples will suffice: H. G. Adams, ed., *God's Image in Ebony; being a series of biographical sketches, facts, anecdotes, etc., demonstrative of the mental powers and intellectual capacities of the Negro race* (London: Partridge and Oakey, 1854), which includes a large section from the earlier work. And in the period of the U.S. Civil Rights movement, a summary version was produced for schoolchildren: Beatrice J. Fleming and Marion J. Pryde, *Distinguished Negroes Abroad* (Washington, D.C.: Associated Publishers, 1946).

According to Debrunner's ample survey, there are no obvious female candidates for consideration in this group. That this should be so is a point in its own right, and reflects the fact that the "white man's burden" of Christian mission, and indeed of ministry generally, was until recent times considered the exclusive domain of men. The scholarly world, too, was very heavily male-dominated in the 18th-century Netherlands. The highly talented Anna Maria van Schurman of Utrecht (1607–1678) was widely known for her knowledge of ancient languages and her philosophical acumen, which are amply displayed in her published writings; yet she remained on the edges of the academic establishment.[5] In terms of gender in the academy, Schurman is eloquent proof of the marginal status of women in the period.

These potted biographies are offered not on the basis of documentary research into the persons concerned but rather as a summary of what might be called a scholarly consensus on each person. As such it should be read with caution. For further reference readers are thus specifically directed to the bibliographies that conclude each entry.

(1) Juan Latino, ca. 1516–1594/97

The origins of Juan Latino, who was to become a professor in Granada, are unclear. We do know that he was captured

---

5. On Schurman, see Schama, *Embarrassment of Riches*, 410–12; Israel, *Dutch Republic*, 671.

"on the Barbary coast" of North Africa, together with his mother, at the age of twelve. It has been speculated that he came from one of North Africa's black Muslim slave households. His studies at the University of Granada were rewarded with a series of degrees: the B.A. in 1546, the Licentiate in 1556, and the M.A. in 1557. Of his many Latin poems to survive, the 900-line *Austriad* is the longest and most familiar. In it he celebrates Don Juan of Austria's victory over the Turkish fleet at Lepanto in 1571. With the help of Don Juan, Latino achieved his freedom and married the noblewoman Doña Ana, by whom he had four daughters. His life story was brought into 19th-century debates on slavery, for he was thought to indicate the academic potential of Africans. In 1935 it was made into a dramatic performance, focusing on his relationship with Doña Ana, and the hindrance initially brought by his slave status.

For further references, see Debrunner, *Presence and Prestige*, 39–40.

(2) Abraham Petrov Hannibal, ca. 1698–1781

The tendency of legends to encrust the lives of African intellectuals is clearly seen in the case of Abraham Petrov Hannibal. He was born to a noble Muslim family in the horn of Africa and originally had the name of Ibrahim. It was only with his baptism in Vilna in 1707 that he took on the name Abraham Petrov. Around 1730 he adopted the name Hannibal, after the famous Carthaginian general who fought against Rome (lived 247–182 B.C.E.).

As a small child of about five or six years Ibrahim was taken away from his home to Istanbul: it is unclear whether he was sold, kidnapped, or sent as part of a tribute to the Sultan. Living in the Seraglio, he was kidnapped or bought by the Russian ambassador on behalf of Tsar Peter I. Under Peter he enjoyed the status of a court favorite, and spent some time studying engineering at Metz, France. He held senior positions in government and the army, but fell out of official favor following Peter's death in 1725. He wrote a treatise on engineering, dedicated to the empress Catherine I. In 1740 he resumed service, rising to a position of authority over all military engineering before his retirement in 1781, at the age of 83.

His first marriage, which was to the daughter of a Greek officer in the Russian army, turned sour at an early stage and eventually ended in divorce. He and his second wife, Christine Sheberg, had twelve children, the third of whom was Ivan Abrahamovich Hannibal, a prominent officer in the Russian army; his grandson was the distinguished Russian poet, Alexander Pushkin (1799–1837). One reason for Hannibal's subsequent fame is that Pushkin wrote about him in his unfinished novel *The Moor of Peter the Great*, which dwells on the erotic complications of his life.

See further Debrunner, *Presence and Prestige*, 115–17; Fleming and Pryde, *Distinguished Negros Abroad*, 166–70. For the novel, see Gillon R. Aitkin, ed., *The Moor of Peter the Great*, in *The Complete Prose Tales of Alexandr Sergeyevitch Pushkin* (London: Barrie and Rockliff, 1966), 3–42.

(3) Francis Williams, ca. 1700–1735

Problems with sources are perhaps most acute in the case of Francis Williams, the Jamaican-born man who studied at Cambridge. As a young child of obvious intelligence, he attracted the attention of the governor of Jamaica, the Duke of Montagu, who had him sent to Britain as a kind of social experiment. Montagu "was struck with the conspicuous talents of this Negro when he was quite young and proposed to try whether, by an improved education, he would be equal to a white man placed in the same circumstances." Williams' subsequent record of study at an English private school and later Cambridge seems to have produced an affirmative answer. In particular, he achieved success in mathematics.

It is to Williams that the eminent Scots philosopher David Hume (1711–1776) refers anonymously in his essay, "Of national characters" (1748). In an endnote Hume alleges that blacks are "naturally inferior to whites." He goes on to claim that blacks are lacking in cultural achievements: "[There are] no ingenious manufactures amongst them, no arts, no sciences." Even those blacks who have found their way to Europe are without real accomplishments, and are thus no exception to the rule: "Not to mention our colonies, there are Negroe slaves dispersed all over Europe, of whom none ever discovered any symptoms of ingenuity. . . In Jamaica, indeed, they talk of one negroe as a man of parts and learning; but it is likely he is admired for slender accomplishments, like a parrot, who speaks a few words plainly." This passage is significant for its theorizing about race, for its language of cultural achievement in doing so, and for its (grudging) recognition of the presence of Africans in Europe.[6]

What little information is available on Williams is summarized in Debrunner, *Presence and Prestige*, 120. Cassirer and Brière's edition of Grégoire, *On the Cultural Achievements of Negroes*, includes a text of the Latin poem composed by Williams, together with an English translation, pages 98–102 and 139–40.

(4) Anton Wilhelm Amo, 1700/1703–ca. 1753

Of all those listed here, Amo has probably attracted the most scholarly attention, as the length of the bibliography below suggests; he was certainly the most prolific writer. A native of Axim in what is today Ghana, Amo is known as the first African to have studied and taught at a German university. He was born to African parents who had con-

---

6. See David Hume, *Political Essays*, ed. Knud Haakonssen (Cambridge: Cambridge University Press, 1994), 86 note f. (My thanks to Professor Simon Gikandi for making me aware of this passage.)

verted to Christianity under the influence of Dutch missionaries. At the age of four he was sent to the Netherlands
to receive a religious education. But he was then presented
by WIC employees to the Duke of Brunswick-Wolfen-
büttel, Anton Ulrich. It was the Duke's patronage that sup-
ported his education in Dutch, German, and French, and in
the ancient languages of Hebrew, Greek, and Latin. In
1727 he went on to study philosophy and jurisprudence at
Halle. His first disputation, "On the rights of Africans in
Europe" (*De jure Maurorum in Europa*, 1729) is now lost,
but from a contemporary description it appears that he
drew on ancient Roman law to challenge the moral legitimacy of the enslavement of Africans in Europe. Unlike
Capitein's thesis, this work does not appear to have drawn
on scripture but purely on the philosophical-legal tradition.

His academic career was most distinguished: from Halle
he moved to Wittenberg, Saxony, for further study, receiving the M.A. degree in 1730 and the Ph.D. in 1734, with a
thesis "On the apathy of the human mind" (*De humanae
mentis apatheia*). This qualified him for the status of lecturer (*Privatdozent*) at the University of Halle in 1736. The
next year he published his major work, the "Treatise on the
art of philosophizing in a sober fashion" (*Tractatus de arte
sobrie philosophandi*), which survives today. In 1739 he left
Halle for Jena.

What he did after 1740 is little known: it is possible that
he took up a position in the Prussian state. Some years
thereafter he returned to Axim. The timing and causes of

his eventual return are not known, but may well be linked with the series of controversies that caused him to change universities on a frequent basis while in Germany. He died in or after 1753, the date of the last traveler's account to mention him.

In philosophy Amo was linked with the Enlightenment rationalism of G. W. Leibniz and Christian Wolff. In his writings on rational psychology (pneumatology), he tried to reconcile tensions between the systems linked with Thomas Aquinas on the one hand and John Locke on the other. Given that Wolff's writings were strongly opposed by the Pietists at Halle, notably A. H. Francke, it is likely that Amo's writings too became embroiled in philosophical and theological conflict. His initial support by the Dukes of Wolfenbüttel came to an end amid these conflicts.

Amo did not marry. A poem with which he declared his love for one Mademoiselle Astrine survives, together with two poems written by her in response, rejecting his advances and mocking his black skin. (These are most accessibly reproduced by R. Bess, pp. 188–92: see below.) It is clear that this story of unrequited love entered the common view of Amo.

At the University of Halle today a major auditorium is named in Amo's honor.

Two of the earliest substantial English-language works on Amo are by Norbert Lochner, "Anton Wilhelm Amo: a Ghana scholar in eighteenth-century Germany," *Transactions of the Historical Society of Ghana* 3 (1958): 169–79;

and William Abraham, "The life and times of Anton Wilhelm Amo," *Transactions of the Historical Society of Ghana* 7 (1964): 60–81.

The most in-depth research on him has been done by Burchard Brentjes in a series of works, beginning with his doctoral thesis: *Antonius Guilielmus Amo Afer aus Axim in Ghana. Student, Doktor der Philosophie Magister legens an den Universitäten Halle, Wittenberg und Jena, 1727–1747. Dokumente, Autographe, Belege* (Halle: Martin-Luther-Universität, 1968). The substance of this work, though not the original documents, went into his subsequent book, *Anton Wilhelm Amo. Der schwarze Philosoph in Halle* (Leipzig: Kochler and Amelang, 1976). Brentjes' article, "Anton Wilhelm Amo in Halle, Wittenberg and Jena," *Universitas* 6 (1977) 39–55, is a translated and shortened version of his earlier piece, "Anton Wilhelm Amo in Halle, Wittenberg und Jena," *Mitteilungen des Instituts für Orientforschung* 15 (1969): 56–76.

Specific aspects are explored by Reginald Bess, "De Jure Maurorum in Europa (On the rights of blacks in Europe): a black civil rights activist in Europe in the Eighteenth Century," in Carol Aisha Blackshire-Belay, ed., *Language and Literature in the African American Imagination*. Contributions in Afro-American and African Studies, vol. 154 (Westport, Conn.: Greenwood, 1992), 181–93; and Paulin J. Hountondji, *African Philosophy: myth and reality*, trans. Henri Evans (Bloomington: Indiana University Press, 1996, 2nd edition), 111–30.

See also John S. Wright's article, "Amo, Anton Wilhelm," in the *Routledge Encyclopedia of Philosophy*, 210–11; and the older account of Debrunner, *Presence and Prestige*, 107–9.

(5) Frederik Pedersen Svane, 1710–1789

Born to an African mother and a Danish father (who died in his first year of life), Frederik Svane studied at the school of the Danish missionary, the Reverend Elias Svane, which was established soon after his arrival in Guinea in 1722. He took the Reverend Svane's name as his own, and came to be known by the Latin name of Fredericus Petri Svane Africanus. He and Christian Protten (discussed below) accompanied the Reverend Svane to Denmark in 1727 when his term as chaplain had come to an end in that year. Soon afterward Frederik was baptized.

For the first five years, the two young men's education consisted of private tuition from the Reverend Svane, with whom they lodged at Sorterup. Frederick Svane enrolled at the University of Copenhagen in 1732, receiving the B.A. degree in 1734. In this same year he married a Danish woman, Maria Badsch. In the course of his studies, he became involved with the Pietist movement; his resulting criticism of the faculty of Divinity led to his expulsion from the university. Inspired by the Pietistic Tranquebar mission, he left for Ghana in 1736 as a missionary in his own right, not attached to any church. Here he was to remain for a decade before returning to Denmark in 1746. This period was marked by various setbacks in his self-motivated mission, including ventures in trading and a spell in prison. His wife had accompanied him, but was soon to return to Denmark; they had one son, who died as a young man in 1757.

After Svane's eventual return, he sought work for some time before being employed as a teacher and deacon (*degn*) in Havrebjerg on the island of Zeeland by the distinguished dramatist Baron Holberg. Here he was for the years 1749 to 1785. He died, following a lengthy illness, in 1789.

The two contemporary accounts of his life are both by Debrunner, in *Evangelisches Missionsmagazin* 101 (1957): 24–31 and *Presence and Prestige*, 84–85.

(6) Christian Jakob Protten, 1715–1769

Protten was born in Christiansborg (Accra-Osu), the son of a Danish father stationed at the Danish Guinea headquarters and a Ghanaian woman who was the sister of a local chief. His native language was Ga, but he also spoke the Akan dialect of Fante. He learned Danish by attending the Castle school run by the Reverend Elias Svane. At the age of 12 he and Frederik Pedersen Svane were chosen by Governor Von Suhm to be schooled in Europe. With Svane he was shortly afterwards baptized at Copenhagen and

enrolled at the university. He left university without completing a degree, returning to Guinea in 1737 under the
auspices of the WIC.

But soon after arriving in Guinea he came into conflict
with the director general, Des Bordes, who had him imprisoned for several years. When Des Bordes left in 1740 and
Protten was released, he returned to Europe, still in the service of the *Broedergemeente*. In the course of his life, Protten in fact was to spend several years in Europe, at Herrn-
hut (1741–42), Marienborg and Copenhagen (1745–56)
and finally Copenhagen (1762–64). A lengthy stay in
Ghana (1756–62) ended when he was linked with the violent death of one of his students, supposedly while cleaning
his gun.

Though Protten's studies in Copenhagen did not bring
him a degree, he did translate a short catechism from
Danish into "Fanteisk og Accraisk" (Akan and Ga), as well
as a brief grammar of those languages. This work survives as
*En nyttig grammatikalsk Indledelse til twende hidintil ganske
unbikiende Sprog, Fanteisk og Accraisk* ("Useful grammatical
introduction to the hitherto completely unknown language
of Fante and Gã," Copenhagen, 1764), and has recently
been translated into English (see below). It underlines the
importance of language as an issue in missionary work, and
proves his practical approach.

See Debrunner's *Presence and Prestige*, 82–83; and his
History of Christianity in Ghana, 62–63, 74–75, 92. For a
reprint of the grammatical treatise, see Christian Protten,

Introduction to the Fante and Accra (Gã) Languages, revised by H. M. J. Trutenau (Gã Dictionary Project Documents and Studies no. 1. Afro-Presse/Luzac: London, 1971).

(7) Philip Quaque, 1741–1816

Relatively easy to reconstruct is the life of Philip Quaque, for whom a substantial body of documents has survived in the archives of the British missionary organization, the *Society for the Promotion of the Gospel* (SPG). Born at the Cape Coast in modern Ghana in 1741, his original name was probably Kwaku ("Wednesday-born"). It was only with his baptism in 1759 that he adopted the name Philip Quaque. At the age of 13 he was sent to Britain together with Thomas Coboro and William Cudjo, the sons of local chiefs, at the prompting of the SPG missionary, the Reverend Thompson.

In Britain the boys studied first with a Mr. Hickman, a schoolteacher based at Islington, either in a private school or in a Parish Charity School. To be sure, their training had a strongly religious element, being centered on reading, writing and the catechism. Shortly after their arrival in Britain they had been examined by the SPG's Committee on their knowledge of the Lord's Prayer and the Apostles' Creed; being favorably impressed, the SPG undertook to finance their tuition. Coboro was to die of consumption in 1758.

In 1757 Quaque and Cudjo were transferred to the care of the Reverend John Moore, a member of the SPG and clergyman at a London church, in order to receive further religious instruction. For seven years the two lived at Moore's home in London. (The view that Quaque studied and was ordained at Oxford, found in some of the older literature, should be rejected.) Cudjo died eight years later, having been confined to a hospital for some time after a mental breakdown.

In 1765 Quaque was ordained as a parish priest, and married the Englishwoman Catherine Blunt, who was of a "modest educational background." He was the first African to be ordained into the Anglican church. A year later, in 1766, he returned to the Cape Coast together with his wife, taking up residence in the Cape Coast Castle. The school he set up was directed at mulatto children in the first instance, but it was also for the children of African merchants. The curriculum was centered on reading, writing, and the catechism; it thus filled a religious function but seems also to have provided the Company of Merchants with African clerks. Enrollment was small, ranging between zero and sixteen with an average of around five, during the years 1766–89. In the light of merely lukewarm support from the SPG, Quaque founded a new Local Education Authority, known as the Torridzonian Society, as a manner of fulfilling the many practical needs he encountered.

English was the language of religious and other instruction. In fact, a surprising feature of the SPG's letters to Quaque was that the Society urged him to "endeavor to recover his own language." The impression given by this, and by his use of an interpreter, is that he was opposed to the use of the vernacular languages, preferring English instead. In this regard, his approach to mission differed markedly from that of the Danish mission at Tranquebar, which made a serious attempt to use the vernacular in spreading the gospel, and from Capitein's efforts to translate the Lord's Prayer, the Articles of Faith, and the Commandments into Fante.

Nonetheless, three general features of his life may be considered common to Capitein's also: religious training for the goal of mission in the motherland; the patronage of wealthy citizens linked with the church in the course of this training; and marriage to a white woman of (probably) low social status.

See further the useful article by F. L. Bartels, "Philip Quaque," *Transactions of the Gold Coast and Togoland Historical Society* 1 (1955): 153–77; Debrunner, *Presence and Prestige*, 81–82.

APPENDIX 3
Capitein and his world: a select bibliography

Bartels, F. L. "Jacobus Eliza Johannes Capitein, 1717–1747," *Transactions of the Historical Society of Ghana* 4 (1959): 3–13. (A still useful account of Capitein's school education at the Hague and his teaching at Elmina.)

Blackburn, Robin. *The Making of New World Slavery: from the Baroque to the modern, 1492–1800*. London: Verso, 1997. (Examines European slave systems in the Atlantic with a view to explaining their role in the advent of modernity.)

Blakely, Allison. *Blacks in the Dutch World: the evolution of racial imagery in a modern society*. Blacks in the Diaspora series. Bloomington: Indiana University Press, 1993. (A brief discussion of Capitein sets him in a context of black intellectuals in the Netherlands and its colonies. Good on artistic representations of blacks.)

Boogart, Ernst van den. "Colour prejudice and the yardstick of civility: the initial Dutch confrontation with black Africans, 1590–1635," in Robert Ross, ed., *Racism and Colonialism: essays on ideology and social structure*. The Hague: Martin Nijhoff, 1982, 33–54. (A nuanced article, showing that the earliest Dutch accounts of the Guinea coast focused on customs rather than on somatic features per se, unlike later reports.)

Boxer, C. R. *The Dutch Seaborne Empire, 1600–1800*. New York: Knopf, 1965. (A seminal and elegantly written work of economic and cultural history.)

Braude, Benjamin. "The sons of Noah and the construction of ethnic and geographical identities in the medieval and early modern periods," *William and Mary Quarterly*, 3rd series 54.1 (1997): 103–42. (Shows the diversity of Jewish and Christian interpretations of Genesis 9 and 10 as a foundational text; proves that the curse of Ham or Canaan was linked with Africa much later than has usually been supposed.)

Davis, David Brion. *The Problem of Slavery in Western Culture*. Ithaca: Cornell University Press, 1966. (A wide-ranging but authoritative intellectual history of the moral perceptions of slavery, spanning European thought from antiquity through the Enlightenment. Still the standard work of its kind.)

Eekhof, A. "De Negerpredikant Jacobus Eliza Johannes Capiteyn," *Nederlandse Archief voor Kerkgeschiedenis*, new series, 13 (1917): 138–74 and 209–76. (An important and lengthy article, making extensive use of original documents, and marking the first serious attempt in the 20th century to make sense of Capitein. Reprints Capitein's correspondence with the WIC and the Classis of Amsterdam as an appendix.)

Emmer, Pieter. *The Dutch in the Atlantic Economy, 1580–1880: trade, slavery and emancipation*. Aldershot: Variorum, 1998. (Includes several important essays, including one comparing the WIC's trading policies with those of the VOC.)

Finkelman, Paul, and Joseph C. Miller, eds. *Macmillan Encyclopedia of World Slavery*. 2 vols. New York: Simon and Schuster, 1998. (A wealth of useful and up-to-date articles ranging extremely widely in slave history; e.g., for current purposes, "Missionaries" by David H. Anthony III.)

Finley, Moses I. *Ancient Slavery and Modern Ideology*. Expanded edition, ed. Brent D. Shaw. Princeton: Markus Wiener, 1998 (orig. 1980). (An important comparative work, reading Greco-Roman slavery and the history of modern scholarship on it against each other.)

Garnsey, Peter. *Ideas of Slavery from Aristotle to Augustine*. Cambridge: Cambridge University Press, 1996. (A thematic examination of selected passages from Greco-Roman authors, including those mentioned by Capitein.)

Grafton, Anthony. "Civic humanism and scientific scholarship at Leiden," in Thomas Bender, ed., *The University and the City: from medieval origins to the present*. New York: Oxford University Press, 1988, 59–78. (An insightful account of Capitein's intellectual milieu at Leiden and the history of that university.)

Huussen, Arend H., Jr. "The Dutch constitution of 1798 and the problem of slavery," in *Tijdschrift voor Rechtsgeschiedenis* 67 (1999): 99–114. (Explores legal manifestations of the moral tension between owning slaves and believing in personal freedom; explains the complete avoidance of the question in the drawing up of the first constitution of the Batavian Republic.)

Israel, Jonathan I. *Dutch Primacy in World Trade, 1585–1740*. Oxford: Clarendon, 1989. (An economic history of Dutch overseas trade, positing seven successive phases.)

Israel, Jonathan. *The Dutch Republic: its rise, greatness, and fall, 1477–1806*. Oxford: Clarendon, 1995. (A monumental work covering a wide range of social, political and economic history.)

Jacob, Margaret C. and Wijnand W. Mijnhardt, eds. *The Dutch Republic in the Eighteenth Century: decline, Enlightenment, and revolution*. Ithaca: Cornell University Press, 1992. (A collection of essays exploring various aspects of political and cultural history.)

de Jong, Gerald Francis. "The Dutch Reformed Church and negro slavery in colonial America," *Church History* 40 (1971): 423–36. (Shows Capitein's views on slavery to have been typical of the contemporary Dutch Reformed Church in the Netherlands, and examines the changing connection between missionary work and slavery.)

Kpobi, David Nii Anum. *Mission in Chains: the life, theology and ministry of the ex-slave Jacobus E. J. Capitein (1717–1747) with a translation of his major publications*. Missiologisch Onderzoek in Nederland series, no. 3. Zoetermeer: Uitgeverij Boekencentrum, 1993. (An in-depth, document-based study of Capitein's life, emphasizing the religious aspects of his life at the expense of others. Translates the dissertation from the Dutch edition, together with letters and sermons, as an appendix.)

Neill, Stephen. *A History of Christian Missions.* Harmondsworth: Penguin, 1986 (orig. 1964). (The standard synthetic work on the subject, though now somewhat dated. Though it fails to mention Capitein, it does help set him in African and Dutch contexts.)

Oostindie, Gert, ed. *Fifty Years Later: antislavery, capitalism and modernity in the Dutch orbit.* Leiden: KITLV, 1994. (An important collection of essays taking as their point of departure Seymour Drescher's piece, "The long goodbye: Dutch capitalism and antislavery in comparative perspective," which is reprinted here.)

Pagden, Anthony. *The Fall of Natural Man: the American Indian and the origins of comparative ethnology.* Cambridge: Cambridge University Press, 2nd ed. 1986 (orig. 1982). (Invaluable account of the ethnological background to Capitein's text, including Aristotle's theory of natural slavery.)

Patterson, Orlando. *Slavery and Social Death: a comparative study.* Cambridge, Mass.: Harvard University Press, 1982. (A seminal work on the comparative sociology of slavery.)

Postma, Johannes Menne. *The Dutch in the Atlantic Slave Trade, 1600–1815.* Cambridge: Cambridge University Press, 1990. (Provides extensive details on the WIC and other aspects of the slave trade. Lengthy appendices of data on the trade.)

Prah, Kwesi Kwaa. *Jacobus Eliza Johannes Capitein, 1717–1747: a critical study of an eighteenth century African.* Trenton, N.J.: Africa World Press, 1992 (orig. Braamfontein, South Africa: Skotaville Publishers, 1989). (A two-hundred-page monograph, impassioned in tone. Includes a valuable account of the history of scholarship about him.)

Price, J. L. *The Dutch Republic in the Seventeenth Century.* New York: St. Martin's Press, 1998. (A brief and well-organized introduction to the historical origins of Capitein's world.)

Thomas, Hugh. *The Slave Trade: the history of the Atlantic slave trade, 1440–1870.* New York: Simon and Schuster, 1997. (Wide-ranging and engagingly written work; though it says relatively little about Dutch slaving, it does allow this to be considered alongside the Iberian, British, and French trade.)

Thornton, John. *Africa and Africans in the Making of the Atlantic World, 1400–1800.* Cambridge: Cambridge University Press, 2nd ed. 1998 (orig. 1992). (Examines early contacts between Portuguese and West Africans, including Congo and Angola; stresses the active involvement of Africans, both in trade with Europeans and as slaves in the New World.)

Wiedemann, Thomas. *Greek and Roman Slavery.* Baltimore: Johns Hopkins University Press, 1981. (Collection of translated passages on Greco-Roman slavery, with brief but authoritative commentary.)

Zee, Henri van der. *'s Heeren Slaaf. Het dramatische leven van Jacobus Capitein.* Amsterdam: Uitgeverij Balans, 2000. (The only recent full-length biography of Capitein.)

155

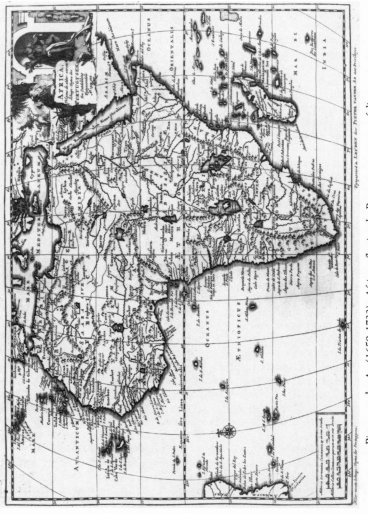

Pieter van der Aa (1659-1733), Africa reflecting the Portuguese voyages of discovery, from Cartes des itineraires et voiages modernes (Leiden 1728). Clements Library, University of Michigan

Abbreviations used in the endnotes

ABD: *Anchor Bible Dictionary* (New York: Doubleday, 1992).

BWN: *Biographisch Woordenboek der Nederland* (Haarlem: Brederode, 1852–1878).

LCL: Loeb Classical Library (Cambridge, Mass.: Harvard University Press).

OCD: *The Oxford Classical Dictionary*, ed. Simon Hornblower and Anthony Spawforth (Oxford: Oxford University Press, 1996, 3rd edition).

REP: *Routledge Encyclopedia of Philosophy* (London: Routledge, 1998).

SHE: *The New Schaff-Herzog Encyclopedia of Religious Knowledge* (Grand Rapids: Baker, 1955).

Note: Biblical quotations and references are to *The Holy Bible: New Revised Standard Version* (New York: Oxford University Press, 1989).

Notes to the Introduction

1. Kwesi Kwaa Prah, *Jacobus Eliza Johannes Capitein, 1717–1747: a critical study of an eighteenth century African* (Trenton: Africa World Press, 1992 [1989]), esp. chapter 1. He begins with an explicit comparison with the story, *Uncle Tom's Cabin, or, Life among the lowly*, written by the philanthropist Harriet Beecher Stowe (1811–1896), and published in serial form in the *National Era*, an antislavery journal based in Washington, D.C. This work was widely read in the years preceding the American Civil War. The point of the comparison is the passive, complaisant image of the main character. Prah, having made the comparison, prefers to modify or even reject it (see e.g. page 2).

2. This essay, as an exercise in intellectual history, owes much to the lead of Quentin Skinner: for critical discussion on the methodological issues at hand, see especially James Tully, ed., *Meaning and Context: Quentin Skinner and his critics* (Cambridge: Polity Press, 1988).

3. On the volume of the trade, Philip D. Curtin, *The Atlantic Slave Trade: a census* (Madison: University of Wisconsin Press, 1969), still provides a point of departure; for discussion and revision, see the essays in David Northrup, ed., *The Atlantic Slave Trade* (Lexington, Mass.: Heath, 1994). Compare most recently the statistics given by David Eltis, *The Rise of African Slavery in the Americas* (Cambridge: Cambridge University Press, 2000).

4. My debt in this biographical section to David Nii Anum Kpobi will become clear: *Mission in Chains: the life, theology and ministry of the ex-slave Jacobus E. J. Capitein* (Uitgeverij Boekencentrum: Zoetermeer, 1993), esp. chapter 2. Compare the monograph of Prah, *Jacobus Eliza Johannes Capitein*. Still useful on specific aspects are A. Eekhof, "De Negerpredikant Jacobus Eliza Johannes Capiteyn," *Nederlandse Archief voor Kerkgeschiedenis* 13 (1917): 138–74 and 209–76, and F. L. Bartels, "Jacobus Eliza Johannes Capitein, 1717–1747," *Transactions of the Historical Society of Ghana* 4 (1959): 3–13. The most detailed recent biography is that by Henri van der Zee, *'s Heeren Slaaf. Het dramatische leven van Jacobus Capitein* (Amsterdam: Balans, 2000).

5. This area was known, while under British control, as the Gold Coast, and now constitutes the independent Republic of Ghana.

6. The treaty was ratified at Münster and at the Hague in the spring of 1648. See further C. R. Boxer, *The Dutch Seaborne Empire, 1600–1800* (New York: Knopf, 1965), 1–3, and Jonathan Israel, *The Dutch Republic: its rise, greatness, and fall, 1477–1806* (Oxford: Oxford University Press, 1995), 596–97.

7. For the prominence of the classical languages in Dutch education at this time, see section III.2 below.

8. Capitein was later to name Cunaeus first among the dedicatees of his dissertation. The fact that he received a bursary from the Hallett Fund from 1737 onward is attested in the records of that organization: see Van der Zee, *'s Heeren Slaaf*, 42.

9. The letters "f" and "s" could be easily confused in 18th-century print and type. For further discussion and references, see Kpobi, *Mission in Chains*, 54. The designation *Afer* was added to the name of the Latin playwright, Terence: see note 56 to the treatise.

10. Kpobi, *Mission in Chains*, 61–62.

11. Despite the claims of several scholars, this does not appear to have been a doctoral dissertation: there is no indication that its conferral was accompanied by the doctoral ceremony. For details see Kpobi, *Mission in Chains*, 66–69.

12. Anthony Grafton, "Civic humanism and scientific scholarship at Leiden," in Thomas Bender, ed., *The University and the City: from medieval origins to the present* (New York: Oxford University Press, 1988), 59–78, at 71.

13. It is as well, on this point, to bear in mind Boxer's emphasis of the subordination of the church (especially missionaries) to the state, at 132–38.

14. As a missionary on the Gold Coast, Capitein does not deserve to have been left out of the standard synthetic account by Stephen Neill, *A History of Christian Missions* (Harmondsworth: Penguin, 1986, 2nd ed. revised by Owen Chadwick), 203. On Capitein the missionary, see Kpobi, *Mission in Chains* (passim) and also Hans W. Debrunner, *A History of Christianity in Ghana* (Accra: Waterville, 1967), 66, 75–76.

15. The New Testament text reads: *For it is the God who said: "Let light shine out of darkness," who has shone in our hearts to give the light of the knowledge of glory of God in the face of Jesus Christ.* In this letter Paul emphasizes the need for the apostles to preach the word of God all over the world. For a translation of Capitein's sermon, see Kpobi, *Mission in Chains*, 220–33: in it Capitein makes extensive reference to light as a symbol and image in this part of the Bible and others.

16. For a text of the letter, see Eekhof, "De Negerpredikant J. E. J. Capiteyn," 246–48; for a translation, Kpobi, *Mission in Chains*, 235.

17. Capitein himself, in a memorandum attached to that same letter of February 15, 1743, addressed to the WIC, takes a grim view of the widespread practice whereby WIC employees would cohabit with indigenous women, some of them mulattoes (*Tapoejers*). For Capitein, the prevalence of this practice, known as *Calacharen*, heightened the need for the education and catechism of local children. The tone of the memorandum is optimistic, and Capitein speaks in glowing terms of the progress already

made in the schooling of 18 or 20 children.

18. On the difficulties of the WIC and the VOC in finding women of the "suitable" social class to send to the colonies, see Boxer, *Dutch Seaborne Empire*, ch. 8, esp. 215–16, 227. Boxer also discusses the practice whereby working-class Dutch women would disguise themselves as men and join VOC crews bound for southeast Asia.

19. The letter of the Classis is dated January 10, 1745: see Kpobi, *Mission in Chains*, 153.

20. Kpobi, *Mission in Chains*, 249–51.

21. Kpobi, *Mission in Chains*, 254.

22. Johannes Menne Postma, *The Dutch in the Atlantic Slave Trade, 1600–1815* (Cambridge: Cambridge University Press, 1990), 71, not unreasonably takes this detail as evidence of alcoholism on Capitein's part.

23. Kpobi, *Mission in Chains*, 77. The comment is all the more striking because there is no obvious evidence of bad feeling between Capitein and Petersen before this.

24. A. van Dantzig, *Het Nederlandse aandeel in de Slavenhandel* (Bussum: Van Dishoeck, 1968), 116, cites no sources in stating baldly that he *did* take part in the slave-trade. On the other hand, Kpobi, *Mission in Chains*, 77, 172, in his discussion of Capitein's debts and trading interests avoids the possibility of Capitein's own slaving.

25. Prah, *J. E. J. Capitein*, 120. For an engaging study of the varied meanings of memory in slave history, with several references to Elmina castle (and modern photographs), see Theresa A. Singleton, "The slave trade remembered on the former Gold and Slave Coasts," *Slavery and Abolition* 20 (1999): 150–69.

26. This, at least, is to follow Equiano's version, which in recent times has been taken at face value. However, a new study has renewed contemporary doubts about his African origins, suggesting instead that he was in born in South Carolina and merely assumed an African identity for rhetorical and financial ends: Vincent Carretta, "Olaudah Equiano or Gustavus Vassa? New light on an eighteenth-century question of identity," *Slavery and Abolition* 20 (1999): 96–105. The evidence deployed by Carretta gives pause, but cannot at present be regarded as conclusive.

27. On this network of topics I am especially indebted to C. R. Boxer, *The Dutch Seaborne Empire*, and Jonathan Israel, *The Dutch Republic*. For a long-term history of West Africa in the Atlantic trade network, stressing the active involvement of Africans, see John Thornton, *Africa and Africans in the Making of the Atlantic World, 1400–1800* (Cambridge: Cambridge University Press, 1998, 2nd edition).

28. There is some disagreement between historians about whether slaves did legally attain their freedom in this manner, or whether Dutch law remained ambiguous on this matter. See for example Seymour Drescher, "The long goodbye: Dutch capitalism and antislavery in compar-

ative perspective," in Gert Oostindie, ed., *Fifty Years Later: Antislavery, capitalism and modernity in the Dutch orbit* (Leiden: KITLV, 1994), 30, esp. n. 13; cf. Richard Elphick and Robert Shell, "Intergroup relations: Khoikhoi, settlers, slaves and free blacks, 1653–1795," in Richard Elphick and Herman Giliomee, eds., *The Shaping of South African Society, 1652–1840* (Middletown: Wesleyan University Press, 1988), 184–239, at 210–11. A recent article outlines the ongoing tension of values and interests in the Netherlands, thus explaining the state's decision to remain silent on the subject of slavery in the colonies when the first constitution of the Batavian Republic was drawn up in 1798: Arend H. Huussen, Jr., "The Dutch constitution of 1798 and the problem of slavery," in *Tijdschrift voor Rechtsgeschiedenis* 67 (1999): 99–114. (I am grateful to Justice Ian Farlam for bringing this important piece to my attention.)

29. Drescher, "The long goodbye." In the case of pre-Revolutionary France, Sue Peabody, *"There are no Slaves in France": the political culture of race and slavery in the Ancien Régime* (New York: Oxford University Press, 1996), shows state attempts to impose unambiguous categories at a time of constant change in the social realities involved. Here too were double standards, for in this period "France was, on the one hand, becoming thoroughly entangled in the Atlantic slave system and, on the other, developing a radical new political discourse based on notions of freedom, equality, and citizenship" (3). On the English Atlantic slave system, compare David Eltis, *The Rise of African Slavery in the Americas*, 1–28.

30. A brief comparison: in Britain it was not until 1772, with the trial of the Virginia-born slave James Somersett, that William Murray, Lord Mansfield established by judicial ruling that an escaped slave could not be forcibly removed from Britain to the colonies. See further, C. R. Boxer, *The Dutch Seaborne Empire, 1600–1800* (New York: Knopf, 1965), 262–63.

31. J. D. Fage, *The History of West Africa: an introductory survey* (Cambridge: Cambridge University Press, 1969 [4th ed.]), 59 and 94; Paul E. Lovejoy, *Transformations in Slavery: a history of slavery in Africa* (Cambridge: Cambridge University Press, 1983), 55–57.

32. Lovejoy, *Transformation in Slavery*, 56; and compare Larry W. Yarak, *Asante and the Dutch, 1744–1873* (Oxford: Clarendon Press, 1990), 99–132, on the mutual dependency of Asante and Dutch commercial interests in the 18th and 19th centuries and their changing relations over time. On the Asante system of great roads in the later period, see esp. Ivor Wilks, *Asante in the Nineteenth Century: the structure and evolution of a political order* (Cambridge: Cambridge University Press, 1975), 1–42.

33. C. R. Boxer, *The Portuguese Seaborne Empire, 1415–1825* (New York: Knopf, 1969), 106–27.

34. For an overall assessment, see esp. Pieter Emmer, "The Dutch and the making of the second Atlantic system," in his collected essays, *The Dutch and the Atlantic Economy, 1580–1880: Trade, slavery and emancipation*

(Aldershot: Variorum, 1998 [orig. 1991]), 11–32. Emmer's use of the two-systems model owes much to Immanuel Wallerstein, *The Modern World-System, I: Capitalist agriculture and the origins of the European world economy in the sixteenth century* (New York: Academic Press, 1974), esp. 199.

35. For a detailed discussion of the architecture of Fort Elmina, still standing today, see A. W. Lawrence, *Trade Castles and Forts in West Africa* (London: Cape, 1969), 103–79; also A. van Dantzig, *Forts and Castles of Ghana* (Accra: Sedco, 1980). On the grim living conditions there in the late 17th century, Hugh Thomas, *The Slave Trade* (London: Picador, 1997), 345–46. As imposing a structure as it was, it did not help the Dutch penetrate the interior, inhabited by the Asante.

36. For an in-depth account of this period in Dutch economic history, see Jonathan Israel, *Dutch Primacy in World Trade, 1585–1740* (Oxford: Clarendon, 1989), 197–291.

37. Postma, *Dutch in the Atlantic Slave Trade*, 17.

38. Both 1441 and 1444 have been claimed as the start of the Atlantic slave trade. In 1441, a Portuguese raiding-party captured ten Africans on the African west coast, near modern Mauritania or southern Morocco. From 1444 regular expeditions brought slaves from Africa's northwestern coast to Portugal for sale; this was the point at which Prince Henry declared the trade in slaves a state monopoly. Up to this point the trade in slaves was largely limited to the Mediterranean itself: the southern capitals of Venice, Seville and Lisbon had been the centers of a flourishing trade in the 14th and 15th centuries. See further Postma, *Dutch in the Atlantic Slave Trade*, 2–3; C. R. Boxer, *Portuguese Seaborne Empire*, 21–22 and 24–25.

39. Postma, *Dutch in the Atlantic Slave Trade*, 10.

40. *The Dutch Republic in the Seventeenth Century* (New York: St. Martin's, 1998), 36.

41. See, in general, Israel, *Dutch Primacy in World Trade*, 377–404, and *Dutch Republic*, 1012–18, stressing the decline of Dutch fine cloth exports. Postma, *Dutch in the Atlantic Slave Trade*, 201–26, describes the period 1730–80 as the "era of free trade," in which Dutch slavers functioned now as middlemen rather than chartered agents for the all-powerful Company.

42. Elmina was in fact the only West African fort the WIC retained in the course of this war: see Israel, *Dutch Republic*, 1097.

43. Here I rely especially on Postma, *Dutch in the Atlantic Slave Trade*, 302–3; compare Lovejoy, *Transformations in Slavery*, 55–57.

44. The disparity between these two figures is explained by the extreme conditions experienced in the so-called "middle passage," whereby slaves would be shipped across the Atlantic amid extreme conditions in which disease was widespread and only the fittest could survive. A mortality rate of 15% in the case of Dutch traders is thus not unusual.

45. The term is taken from Simon Schama's *Embarrassment of Riches: an interpretation of Dutch culture in the Golden Age* (New York: Simon and

Schuster, 1987); chapter 5, dealing with social relations generally and out-
siders in particular, is most relevant to the current discussion. On the slave
trade compare Israel, *Dutch Republic*, 307.

46. Sir William Temple, the British ambassador, had this to say in 1668:
"their men of war are manned by mariners of all nations, who are very
numerous among them, but especially those of the eastland coasts of
Germany, Swedes, Danes, and Norwegians." See his *Observations upon the
United Provinces of the Netherlands* (London: Gellibrand, 1673, 2nd ed.),
183.

47. Postma, *Dutch in the Atlantic Slave Trade*, 302.

48. Boxer, *Dutch Seaborne Empire*, 209.

49. Boxer, *Dutch Seaborne Empire*, 205.

50. Postma, *Dutch in the Atlantic Slave Trade*, 70.

51. Compare notes 16 and 17 above.

52. Boxer, *Dutch Seaborne Empire*, 257.

53. Here I take a position between the extremes represented on the one
hand by Prah (*J. E. J. Capitein*), who writes Capitein off as an Uncle Tom
and a dupe of his Dutch masters, thus minimizing his agency, and on the
other hand Kpobi (*Mission in Chains*), whose perspective is very predomi-
nantly theological and missiological, and subordinates economic issues to
religious ones.

54. Boxer, *Dutch Seaborne Empire*, 134.

55. The summary offered here quite deliberately glosses over the many
difficulties of interpretation implicit in the Genesis passage: they are of no
immediate relevance to Capitein's use of the biblical story. Strictly speaking, it is Ham's son, Canaan, that is cursed: "Cursed be Canaan! The low-
est of slaves will he be to his brothers" (Gen. 9:25). This is just one of the
problems of interpretation involved in this passage, with its probable con-
fluence of traditions and its long history of exegesis. It appears that the
point of the story is Ham's disrespectfulness: upon seeing his father in this
state, he did nothing more than report the fact to his brothers, who did on
the other hand take steps to restore his dignity. Other interpretations have
presented Ham as castrating or assaulting his father, but these are not con-
vincing. At all events, biblical scholars have taken the story as a legitima-
tion of Israel's conquest (or impending conquest) of Canaan around the
start of the 12th century B.C.E.

In subsequent centuries its somatic element (the black skin of Ham's
descendants) has made it into a ready justification for the oppression of
Africans. On the problems involved see for example, E. A. Speiser, ed.,
Genesis. The Anchor Bible (New York: Doubleday, 1964), 60–63; Ephraim
Isaac, "Ham," *Anchor Bible Dictionary* (New York: Doubleday, 1992). In a
fine article, Benjamin Braude, "The sons of Noah and the construction of
ethnic and geographical identities in the medieval and early modern periods," *William and Mary Quarterly*, 3rd series 54.1 (1997): 103–42, shows

that it was not until late (the 18th century) that "Ham" was consistently identified with Africa rather than Asia.

56. Pontoppidan, in defending slavery, argued that however bad conditions were in the Americas, they were worse still on the African continent. He regarded the prospects of missionary activity in Africa as hopeless, and hence, "for my purpose it is enough that the said negro approaches the Light [i.e. God] at least there [in the Caribbean], rather than in his native country." For detailed discussion, see Sv. E. Green-Pedersen, "Negro slavery and Christianity: on Erik Pontoppidan's preface to L. F. Roemer['s] *Tilforladelig Efterretning om Kysten Guinea* (A true account of the coast of Guinea), 1760," *Transactions of the Historical Society of Ghana* 15 (1974): 85–102, at 86.

57. For the use of the Bible in antebellum North America to justify slavery, see Davis, *The Problem of Slavery in the Age of Revolution*, 523–56.

58. Sanford Budick and Wolfgang Iser, eds., *The Translatability of Cultures: figurations of the space between* (Stanford: Stanford University Press, 1996); James Clifford, *Routes: travel and translation in the late twentieth century* (Cambridge, Mass.: Harvard University Press, 1997).

59. R. E. O. Ekkart, *Nederlandse portretten uit de 17e eeuw. Dutch Portraits from the Seventeenth Century* (Rotterdam: Museum Boymans-van Beuningen, 1995), 188–90.

60. Blakely, *Blacks in the Dutch World*, 78–170.

61. See p. 96 in the edition by Paul Edwards, ed., *Equiano's Travels: his autobiography. The Interesting Narrative of the Life of Olaudah Equiano or Gustavus Vassa the African* (London: Heinemann, 1967). For a detailed study, see James Walvin, *An African's Life: the life and times of Olaudah Equiano, 1745–1797* (London: Cassell, 1998).

62. As Capitein says just earlier, "miraculously guided by God, we sailed over [from Guinea] and arrived at Middelburg."

63. Faith, hope, and charity (or love: *agape* in Greek) are the gifts of the Holy Spirit, according to the apostle Paul in I Corinthians 13:13. These have very frequently been taken to sum up the entire essence of Christianity, and this is the function they serve in the poem quoted.

64. The portrait is entitled "Jacobus Elisa Joannes Capitein, Africaansche Moor. Beroepen Predikant aan het Kasteel st. George op D'Elmina." The poem runs: "Aanschouwer zie deez' Moor: zijn vel is zwart, maar wit / zijn ziel, daar Jesus zelf als Priester voor hem bidt. // Hij gaat Geloof en Hoop en Liefde aan Mooren leeren, / Opdat zij, witgemaakt, met hem het Lam steeds eeren." See p. 48.

65. For a powerful demonstration of changing interpretations of a foundational and seemingly familiar text, see Braude, "The sons of Noah."

66. For details, including references, see Kpobi, *Mission in Chains*, 16–18 and 260; and compare appendix 2 below. Much of the interest in him in the Netherlands and in Germany in the 18th and 19th centuries seems to

have been fascination with a *Kulturkuriosum*—in a word, the paradox of the learned African. Note, for example, the two short articles under the title "Afrikaan in de vorige eeuw tot Theologiae Doctor gepromoveerd," by J. van der Baan and A. J. van Aa, in *Navorschers Bijblad* 5 (1855): 71–72 and 146 respectively. These are merely two of ten short pieces on Capitein from the 1850s through the 1870s identified by Kpobi, *Mission in Chains*.

67. On the afterlife of Roman rhetoric, see for example George A. Kennedy, "Rhetoric," in Richard Jenkyns, ed., *The Legacy of Rome: a new appraisal* (Oxford: Oxford University Press, 1992), 269–94, esp. 291.

68. The Latin schools were restricted to boys, unlike the elementary schools. On these schools, see Boxer, *Dutch Seaborne Empire*, 156. The curriculum of the various Latin schools was standardized by law in 1625, Latin taking up twenty to thirty hours per week in the first three years, and between ten and eighteen hours in the final years, whereupon Greek would also be taught.

69. On this siege and the remarkable feat whereby the Dutch relieved it, see Schama, 26–28; on the establishment of the university, Boxer, *Dutch Seaborne Empire*, 31, 65.

70. Maria Wilhelmina Jurriaanse, *The Founding of Leyden University* (Leiden: Brill, 1965), 5.

71. For an attempt to characterize the institution, in its complex and often contradictory aspects, see Anthony Grafton, "Civic humanism and scientific scholarship at Leiden," in Thomas Bender, ed., *The University and the city: from medieval origins to the present* (New York: Oxford University Press, 1988), 59–78, with considerable bibliography. On the international professoriate, see esp. J. J. Woltjer, "Foreign professors," in Th. H. Lunsingh Scheurleer and G. H. M. Posthumus Meyjes, eds., *Leiden University in the Seventeenth Century: an exchange of learning* (Leiden: Brill, 1975), 461–65.

72. See further Boxer, *Dutch Seaborne Empire*, 158–59; D. W. Davies, *The World of Elseviers, 1580–1712* (The Hague: Nijhoff, 1954), offers many insights into the Dutch academic world inhabited by Capitein.

73. The following extract points to Voltaire's implied criticism of both the church and of slavery. The hero, Candide, on his adventures in the New World, encounters an African man lying on the ground, dressed only in a pair of canvas trousers, lacking both a left leg and a right hand. Speaking in Dutch, Candide asks the man why he is there, in such a wretched state.

"I am waiting for my master, Mr. Vanderdendur, who owns the famous sugar-works," replied the negro.

"Did Mr. Vanderdendur treat you like this?" asked Candide.

"Yes, Sir," said the negro, "it's the custom. For clothing, we are given a pair of canvas drawers twice a year. Those of us who work in the factories and happen to catch a finger in the grindstone have a hand chopped off; if we try to escape, they cut off one leg. Both accidents happened to me.

That's the price of your eating sugar in Europe. My mother sold me on the coast of Guiana for fifty Spanish shillings. . . . Dogs, monkeys, and parrots are much less miserable than we are. The Dutch fetishes, who converted me, tell every Sunday that we are all children of Adam, black and white alike. I am no genealogist; but if these preachers speak the truth, we must all be cousins. Now, you will surely agree that relations could not be treated more horribly."

Voltaire, *Candide, or Optimism*, translated by John Butt (Harmondsworth: Penguin, 1947), 85–86.

74. The treatise *Airs, waters, places* in the large body of medical texts attributed to Hippocrates (5th century B.C.E.) enunciates the theory that particular kinds of environment determine certain somatic features, which are in effect the mark of their inhabitants. Thus, to simplify, a harsh, cold climate such as that of south-eastern Europe inspires a warlike disposition in the Scythians, whereas elsewhere warm weather makes a region's inhabitants lazy and docile; the temperate lands of the Aegean world, on the other hand, gives the Greeks an ideal constitution. This approach, already well established in the classical Greek period of Hippocrates, Herodotus, and Plato, was to have enormous impact in later centuries. On the considerable afterlife of this idea see Davis, *The Problem of Slavery in Western Culture* (Ithaca: Cornell University Press, 1966), 414–16.

75. On the contradictory positions held by Enlightenment philosophers concerning slavery, see, for example, Moses I. Finley, *Ancient Slavery and Modern Ideology* (Princeton: Markus Wiener Publishers, 1998, expanded ed., ed. Brent D. Shaw), 87–89.

76. Boxer, *Dutch Seaborne Empire*, 185.

77. Pieter Emmer presents the Netherlands as "catching up with the rest of Europe" in the growth of anti-slavery sentiment: "Anti-slavery and the Dutch: abolition without reform," in *The Dutch in the Atlantic Economy, 1580–1880* (Aldershot: Variorum, 1998 [1980]), 127–44.

78. For a critical synthesis of different strands within Greco-Roman thought, through the church fathers, see especially Peter Garnsey, *Ideas of Slavery from Aristotle to Augustine* (Cambridge: Cambridge University Press, 1996). This and Thomas Wiedemann's annotated collection, *Greek and Roman Slavery* (Baltimore: Johns Hopkins University Press, 1981) discuss most of the classical texts deployed by Capitein in their original contexts. Ideological issues surrounding slavery in the (non-Christian) Roman world are analyzed by William Fitzgerald, *Slavery and the Roman Literary Imagination* (Cambridge: Cambridge University Press, 2000).

79. David Brion Davis, *Problem of Slavery in Western Culture*, e.g. 217, 316–17; and on the later period, *The Problem of Slavery in the Age of Revolution* (Ithaca: Cornell University Press, 1975), 539–41, 555–56. Also, Robin Blackburn, *The Making of New World Slavery* (London: Verso, 1997), 64–76.

80. Paul requests that the runaway slave Onesimus, whom he had got to know while both were imprisoned, receive lenient treatment from his master Philemon. "Onesimus" was a common Greek slave-name meaning "useful."

81. For references with some discussion, see I. A. H. Combes, *The Metaphor of Slavery in the Writings of the Early Church from the New Testament to the Beginning of the Fifth Century* (Sheffield: Sheffield Academic Press, 1998), esp. 68–94. More analytical is Dale B. Martin, *Slavery as Salvation: the metaphor of slavery in Pauline Christianity* (New Haven: Yale University Press, 1990).

82. *His state was divine, yet he did not cling to his equality with God / but emptied himself to assume the condition of a slave, and became as men are; and being as all men are, / he was humbler yet, even to accepting death, death on a cross.* This is from a hymn within the letter, and it is unclear whether the hymn was composed by Paul himself.

83. I Corinthians 7:20–23, which is worth quoting in full: *Let everyone stay as he was at the time of his call. If, when you were called, you were a slave, do not let this bother you; but if you should have the chance of being free, accept it. A slave, when he is called in the Lord, becomes the Lord's freedman, and a freedman called in the Lord becomes Christ's slave. You have all been bought and paid for; do not be slaves of other men.*

84. William J. Bouwsma, *John Calvin: a sixteenth century portrait* (New York: Oxford University Press, 1988), 34–35.

85. On the centrality of the Bible (alongside the Greek and Latin classics) to the cosmologies of the first Europeans in the Americas, see, for example, Anthony Grafton, *New Worlds, Ancient Texts: the power of tradition and the shock of discovery* (Cambridge, Mass.: Harvard University Press, 1992). Anthony Pagden, *The Fall of Natural Man: the American Indian and the origins of comparative ethnology* (Cambridge, England: Cambridge University Press, 1986, 2nd ed. [1982]), includes a chapter on early modern critiques of Aristotle's theory of natural slavery. His introduction to Bartolomé de Las Casas, *A Short Account of the Destruction of the Indies*, tr. Nigel Griffin (Harmondsworth: Penguin, 1992), provides a lucid and rich introduction to the topic. For an idiosyncratic but thoughtful reading of the debate between Las Casas and Sepúlveda, see Tzvetan Todorov, *The Conquest of America: the question of the other* (New York: Harper, 1992 [1982]), 151–77. Davis, *Problem of Slavery in Western Culture*, esp. 446, presents the 1760s as the period which saw the weakening of biblical and classical sanctions on slavery.

86. In fact Las Casas' treatise was translated into Dutch and used as proof of the brutality of the Spanish, in keeping with antipathy toward Spain as a colonizing power in the 17th-century Netherlands. See further Schama, *Embarrassment of Riches*, 84.

87. One of the differences between the two was Sepúlveda's adherence

167

to Aristotle, and particularly his theory of natural slavery: Grafton, *New Worlds, Ancient Texts*, 136.

88. Esp. book 19, ch. 15. Augustine writes that humankind, in Genesis' creation narrative, was born free, and put in a position of authority over the rest of creation; the advent of slavery is the direct result of human sinfulness. "[God] did not wish the rational being, made in his own image, to have dominion over any but irrational creatures, not man over man, but man over the beasts. Hence the first just men were set up as shepherds of flocks, rather than as kings of men, so that in this way also God might convey the message of what was required by the order of nature, and what was demanded by the deserts of sinners—for it is understood, of course, that the condition of slavery is justly imposed on the sinner. That is why we do not hear of slaves anywhere in the scriptures until Noah, the just man, punished his son [Ham]'s sin with the word; and so that son deserved his name because of his misdeed, not because of his nature." (translated by Henry Bettenson, Harmondsworth, 1972, page 874). In the light of these comments, it is clear why Augustine (and later Capitein) differed from Aristotle's theory of "natural slavery." For further commentary on the Augustine passage, see further Garnsey, 208–10. Peter Brown, *Augustine of Hippo* (Berkeley: University of California Press, 1967), 388, shows that the idea of original sin was widespread in the fourth century.

89. See Davis, 291–332, on the antislavery position of Quakers and its debt to earlier British Protestantism; also Davis, *Problem of Slavery in the Age of Revolution*, 213–54.

90. Capitein's "theological" ethnology of Africans *tout court*, permeated by this color-symbolism, could not be more different from the first chapters of Equiano's *Interesting Narrative*, in which he describes his native area of Nigeria in terms that recall a detailed traveler's account—except that he uses the first person plural, "we" and "us," as if he goes to great lengths to make sense of life in Nigeria to his British readership. See further Walvin, *An African's Life*, 4–14.

91. The identification of Africans with sin, based on a long-standing conception of blackness as evil, is explicit in a variety of ancient texts, and is well entrenched by the time of the Roman representations described by Lloyd A. Thompson, *Romans and Blacks* (London: Routledge, 1989), 110–13. Early Christian writers were amenable to this use of imagery. See also Davis, *Problem of Slavery in Western Culture*, 446–82, and V. Y. Mudimbe, *The Idea of Africa* (Bloomington: Indiana University Press, 1994), 71–104, on the persistence of ancient imagery into the early modern period.

92. Note for example Stephen Neill, *A History of Christian Missions*, 14.

93. Debrunner, *History of Christianity in Ghana*, 61.

94. On Velse, see the valuable discussion by Kpobi, *Mission in Chains*, 56–58 and esp. 86–88.

95. *Codex Theodosianus* 4.7.1: see Wiedemann, *Greek and Roman Slavery*, 50–51. Insofar as the practice was followed, this type of manumission took place at Easter worship, provided the slave had served for six years.

96. Drescher, "The long goodbye," 58.

97. Postma, *Dutch in the Atlantic Slave Trade*, 292–93; cf. Drescher, 58.

98. A. N. Paasman, *Reinhart: Nederlandse Literatuur en Slavernij ten tijde van de Verlichting* (Leiden: Nijhoff, 1984), esp. 27. For other instances and further references, see Gerald Francis de Jong, "The Dutch Reformed Church and negro slavery in colonial America," *Church History* 40 (1971): 423–36; J. M. van der Linde, *Jan Willem Kals, Leraar der Hervormden, advocaat van indiaan en neger* (Kampen: Kok, 1987); Gerrit J. Schutte, "Bij het schemerlicht van hun tijd. Zeventiende-eeuwse gereformeerden en de slavenhandel," in M. Bruggeman, ed., *Mensen van de Nieuwe Tijd: een liber amicorum voor A. Th. van Deursen* (Amsterdam: Bert Bakker, 1996), 193–216.

99. The Dutch original reads: "Onmenschelyck ghebruyck! Godeloose schelmery! / Dat men de menschen vent, tot paartsche slaverny! / Hier zynder oock in stadt, die sulcken handel dryven, / In Farnabock: maar't sal Godt niet verhoolen blyven." See Paasman, *Reinhart*, 116. Farnabock was the Dutch name for Pernambuco in Brazil.

100. See Postma, *Dutch in the Atlantic Slave Trade*, 11.

101. Note especially Seymour Drescher's essay, "The long goodbye: Dutch capitalism and antislavery in comparative perspective," in Oostindie, ed., *Fifty Years Later* (1996), together with the essays in that volume critiquing it.

102. Originally used by Emmer, "Antislavery and the Dutch," 127: this gave the impetus to the subsequent use by Drescher and Bender.

103. Drescher, "Long goodbye," 66; cf. Angelie Sens, "Dutch antislavery attitudes in a decline-ridden society, 1750–1815," also in Oostindie, ed., *Fifty Years Later*, 89–104, at 90.

104. In the face of this challenge, the Synod upheld the orthodox Reformed view, championed by Franciscus Gomarus and others, that predestination is not conditional on belief; among many other matters of the faith, the Synod also reaffirmed the sinful nature of humankind.

105. Israel, *Dutch Republic*, 4, 183.

106. Israel, *Dutch Republic*, 677–99, in his chapter entitled "Freedom and order," writes of the complexities involved in the "freedom" of the Dutch: he does well to stress that the personal freedom of individuals was directly linked with wider, often unspoken community-wide checks and balances, i.e. modes of social discipline and control.

107. Drescher, "The long goodbye," 52–53.

108. Sir William Temple, *Observations upon the United Provinces of the Netherlands* (London: Gellibrand, 1673, 2nd edition), 170.

109. Sheila D. Muller, *Charity in the Dutch Republic: Pictures of rich and*

poor for charitable institutions (Ann Arbor, Mich.: UMI Research Press, 1985), well documents the prominence with which charity was commemorated in the Dutch Golden Age. One new development was the 17th-century vogue for group portraits of regents of charitable houses; in general, the emphasis tends to fall on generous benefactors more than on impoverished recipients.

110. See, for example, Finley, *Ancient Slavery and Modern Ideology*, 141.

111. Orlando Patterson, *Slavery and Social Death: a comparative study* (Cambridge, Mass.: Harvard University Press, 1982): "slavery is the permanent, violent domination of natally alienated and generally dishonored persons" (13). For the limitations of viewing slavery as property see pp. 21–27. Closely related to Patterson's approach is the definition of slavery as the "institutionalization of marginality" discussed by David Brion Davis, *Slavery and Human Progress* (New York: Oxford University Press, 1984), 14.

Notes to Capitein's dissertation

112. Japheth and Ham are two of Noah's three sons, the other being Shem. Ham and his progeny are cursed by Noah after Ham finds him lying drunken and naked (presumably because he fails to conceal Noah's shame). In keeping with the curse, Ham's son Canaan is to become the slave of Japheth (Gen. 9:20–27). On the centrality of this story to Capitein's ethnology and theology, and on some of the difficulties surrounding its interpretation, see section IV.1 of the introduction above.

113. The Covenant or Dispensation is a central doctrine of Christianity, and one that establishes its relationship with Judaism. God's covenant with Noah, following the flood, binds God with all creatures, human and animal, in a set of mutual promises and obligations (Genesis 9:1–17). Specifically, the law God gives to Moses on Mount Sinai is referred to as a covenant (Exodus 24:7). At a number of other significant passages in the Old Testament the term covenant (Hebrew *berit*) denotes God's relationship with humans, based on the law given to Moses.

In the Christian tradition it is Jesus, as God's son, who supersedes the law and thus establishes anew God's relationship with humans. The contrast is most piquantly expressed in Paul's second letter to the Corinthians 3:4–11. According to Paul, the law given to Moses was a *ministry of death* (v. 7) because it was temporary and provisional, whereas the New Covenant in Christ is for all time (v. 11).

114. *Once you were not a people, but now you are God's people* (I Peter 2:10); *For the promise is for you, for your children, and for all who are far away, everyone whom the Lord our God calls to him* (Acts 2:39: part of Peter's call to the Jews of Jerusalem to repent).

115. This passage is from the eschatology (description of the end of time) contained in the prophecy of Zechariah, dating to 520–518 B.C.E. As foretold here, Jerusalem will suffer but is defended by God from total destruction.

116. "The river" may be understood as the Euphrates, as is established at I Kings 4.21.

117. The ancient figures mentioned here were considered leaders of the church in the immediate aftermath of the apostles. Timothy and Titus were at different times Paul's companions on his travels, and were later to be missionaries in their own right (e.g. Acts 16:1–5 and Galatians 2:1–3 respectively). They are the recipients of three brief letters included in the New Testament, namely I and II Timothy and Titus. These epistles, known from the practical nature of their content as pastoral letters, have traditionally been ascribed to Paul, though stylistic criteria would suggest that they were written by someone else.

Clement of Rome was probably identical with Pope Clement (around 90–100 C.E.). The letter from the church at Rome to the church in Corinth that is usually ascribed to him presents a Christian community that has settled down by the end of the first century C.E., and is no longer urgently concerned with the impending end of time.

Polycarp (ca. 69–ca. 155) was bishop of Smyrna from 110 to his death by martyrdom. Of his writings only one letter that he wrote to the Philippians, which might originally have been two letters, survives. It warns against apostasy, i.e. renunciation of the faith on the part of Christians.

Quadratus (early 2nd century C.E.) was the first of the Christian "apologists." While based in Asia Minor he wrote a defense of Christianity addressed to the Roman emperor Hadrian (r. 117–138). Only one fragment of the work survives; it is contained in the church history of Eusebius (ca. 260–ca. 340).

Ignatius (d. 108 or 115) was born in Antioch. Condemned to death there for his Christian allegiance, he was sent to Rome to be thrown to the beasts. His own letters, written en route there to Christian churches in various parts of the eastern Mediterranean, are the main source of information about him. It is unclear whether he did finally endure martyrdom. His letters warn against heresy and exhort Christians to unite under the bishop and clergy. Their shrill tone is in marked contrast to that of Clement, with whom he corresponded.

William Cave (1637–1713): British patristic scholar who wrote voluminously on the history of the church. See SHE vol. 3.461. It would appear that Cave's work was Capitein's major source on these authors.

118. At this passage paraphrased by Capitein, Jesus, instructing the twelve apostles to spread the Gospel, says: Go *nowhere among the Gentiles and enter no town of the Samaritans, but go rather to the lost sheep of the house of Israel.*

119. Gaius Maecenas (d. 8 C.E.) was classical Rome's most famous literary patron. A counsellor of the emperor Augustus, he was associated with the most distinguished poets of the time, including Virgil and Horace (on whom, see notes 169 and 133 below). From ancient times his name became a byword for the ideal literary patron.

120. If *Capitein* was the name Van Goch chose for the slave-boy, it might indeed be explained on the basis that he was a gift from sea-captain, Steenhart: thus Kpobi, *Mission in Chains*, 190. At the same time, however, there may be a note of sarcasm in calling a slave "captain": on the use of facetious names for slaves, though in a different part of Africa, see Robert C.-H. Shell, *Children of Bondage: a social history of slave society at the Cape of Good Hope, 1652–1838* (Johannesburg: Witwatersrand University Press, 1994), 240–41, where the most piquant example cited, Fortune (*Fortuijn*), also reverses the roles of master and slave in playful fashion.

121. The story of Naomi and Elimelech is told in the Old Testament book of Ruth. They were a married couple, who left Bethlehem for Moab together with their sons, at a time of famine. Elimelech died, and their sons married Moabite women (one of whom is Ruth), but then died also. Naomi then returned to Bethlehem, together with the loyal Ruth, who after her subsequent marriage to Boaz became the grandmother of King David. Capitein refers to the story here as a paradigmatic instance of conjugal love, and the loss of a husband. See further ABD, "Naomi."

122. Nestor was a hero of Greek mythology, among those fighting in the Trojan War and later returning from it. Famed for his longevity, he is presented as an elder statesman figure in Homer's *Iliad*. See further OCD, "Nestor."

123. The Styx ("abominable") was the main river of Hades, the underworld of Greek mythology. The souls of the dead had to cross this river in order to reach their final resting place. It is interesting to note the juxtaposition of the (pagan) classical with the Christian at this point. See further OCD, "Styx."

124. Mount Olympus, the highest mountain of Greece, situated on its northern border, was considered the home of the twelve "Olympian" gods. See further OCD, "Olympus."

125. Ambrosia was a mythical food considered to confer immortality on humans.

126. Nothing more is known about Roscam. It is significant, however, to see her compared with Anna Maria Schurman in an account of Capitein from the early 19th century: see Henri Grégoire, *On the Cultural Achievements of Negroes*, tr. and ed. Thomas Cassirer and Jean-François Brière (Amherst: University of Massachusetts Press, 1996), 94. For more on Schurman (and Grégoire), see Appendix 2 below.

127. Marcus Tullius Cicero (106–43 B.C.E.): Roman statesman, orator, writer on various subjects, not least philosophical. The three books of his treatise *De officiis* ("on duties"), written in the last year of his life, may be consulted in the bilingual edition of Walter Miller, LCL series (1913). For a detailed study of this work, see Andrew R. Dyck, *A Commentary on Cicero, De Officiis* (Ann Arbor: University of Michigan Press, 1996). The canonical status of Cicero in Capitein's scholarly world is underlined by the fact that, at the elaborate ceremony to mark the inauguration of the university in 1575, he was represented in the procession, along with Aristotle, Plato and Virgil, and following the four Evangelists, four Roman jurists and four Greek and Roman medical writers: see Maria Wilhelmina Jurriaanse, *The Founding of Leyden University* (Leiden: Brill, 1965), 10, with contemporary illustration.

128. Lucius Annaeus Seneca, Seneca the younger (3 B.C.E.–65 C.E.), Roman statesman, philosopher, and poet, was very influential for the later history of Stoic philosophy. In medieval manuscripts, brief quotes of a

moralising nature from his tragedies become mixed in with texts of Publi-lius Syrus, a writer of mimes (popular entertainments for the stage) who came to Rome as a slave in the mid-1st century B.C.E., probably from Antioch. The apophthegms (moralising maxims) from these mimes were used in the education of Roman schoolboys as a kind of fund of proverbial wisdom. The edition referred to by Capitein is that of Jan Gruter (Janus Gruterus, 1560–1627).

129. Aristotle (384–321 B.C.E.): Greek philosopher and founder of the Peripatetic school; in his treatise, *Politics*, he was the originator of the very influential theory of natural slavery. On this much-quoted passage, see the discussion in T. Wiedemann, *Greek and Roman Slavery: a sourcebook* (Baltimore: Johns Hopkins University Press, 1981), 15–21; P. Garnsey, *Ideas of Slavery from Aristotle to Augustine* (Cambridge: Cambridge University Press, 1996), 35–38, 107–127. Among the many translations of the work, see especially Stephen Everson, *Aristotle: The Politics* (Cam-bridge: Cambridge University Press, 1988).

130. Apart from his tragedies mentioned above, Seneca also wrote *Letters*, which are in effect essays on subjects of ethical philosophy. See Seneca, *Ad Lucilium Epistulae Morales*, vol. 1 (LCL vol. 4), trans. Richard M. Gunmere, p. 229.

131. Odoardus Bisetus: 17th-century commentator on Aristophanes (ca. 445–ca. 385 B.C.E.), the classical Greek world's pre-eminent writer of comedies. See Bisetus' copiously annotated edition, *Aristophanis comoediae undecim* (1607).

132. Constantine Harmenopoulos (d. 1380): Compiled a "corpus" or body of secular and canon law, thus organising legal material into a new system which was more easily used. In so doing he created a legal code that was extensively used in Greece and certain Slavic countries until fairly recently. A partial translation is available in Edwin Hanson Freshfield, *Konstantinos Hermenopoulos: a manual of Byzantine law* (Cambridge: Cambridge University Press, 1930).

133. Horace, Quintus Horatius Flaccus (65–8 B.C.E.): Roman poet who wrote both lyric and satirical verse, in the second part of his life under the reign of Augustus. For detailed modern commentary on this passage see R. G. M. Nisbet and Margaret Hubbard, *A Commentary on Horace*, Odes I (Oxford: Clarendon, 1970).

134. Capitein proceeds at this point to cite Harmenopoulos' definition, already given a few lines above, the difference being that in the earlier pas-sage Capitein quotes the original Greek, whereas here he translates it into Latin. Note also the quotations from Hebrew in chapters 3–7 below, the original Hebrew characters being used in each case.

135. Alcimus Avitus (ca. 490–518): bishop of Vienne, France, and opponent of the Arian heresy. The work referred to is his biblical epic *De spiritalis historiae gestis*, in five books, in which themes from the Genesis nar-

rative are put into Virgilian verse. A scholar of Capitein's time would probably have been familiar with the 1677 edition from Lyons: see Daniel J. Nodes, ed., *Saint Avitus: The fall of man* (Toronto: Center for Medieval Studies, 1985), 1–10, 62–64.

136. Athenaeus (flourished ca. 200 C.E.): His only extant work, the compendious *Deipnosophists*, in which various topics of philosophy, literature, law, medicine and the like are discussed over several days at a learned banquet. Greek text and parallel English translation are available in the LCL series, edited by C. B. Gulick (7 vols., 1927–41).

Ammonius of Alexandria, also known as Ammonius Saccas: Platonist philspher who flourished in the first half of the 3rd century C.E. Among his many students was the prolific Plotinus. It is possible that he was brought up a Christian. Though various stories have attached themselves to his name since late antiquity, the nature and extent of his own contribution can only be conjectured. In 1739, just three years before Capitein delivered his lecture, an edition of Ammonius had been published under the title *De differentia adfinium vocabulorum* by the distinguished scholar, Lodewyk Kaspar Valckenaer (1715–1785), then professor of Greek at the University of Franeker and later to hold the chair at Leiden (1766–85). This was most likely the edition consulted by Capitein.

137. In Leviticus 25:39–55 God instructs the Israelites that they may never become slaves, though they may sell themselves as hired servants if circumstances demand it. *For they are my servants, whom I brought out of the land of Egypt; they shall not be sold as slaves are sold.* (42) However, the passage goes on to say that they are allowed to makes slaves out of non-Israelites, since they are considered to be outside the covenant community: *As for the male and female slaves whom you may have, it is from the nations around you that you may acquire male and female slaves. You may also acquire them from among the aliens residing with you, and from their families that are with you, who have been born in your land; and they may be your property.* (verses 44–45). It is this, second aspect of the Leviticus chapter that Capitein has in mind when he cites it, as is made clear a little later, at paragraph 7 of his treatise.

138. Laurentius Pignorius (1571–1631), also known as Lorenzo Pignoria, studied at Padua and Rome. His treatise on ancient slavery and other kinds of labor, *De servis et eorum apud veteres ministeriis commentarius* (1613), may be considered the first piece of humanist scholarship to deal specifically with slavery as an institution of ancient Greeks and Romans. Like Capitein, he too disagreed with Aristotle's theory of natural slavery. See further Joseph Vogt's piece, "Slavery and the Humanists," in his collected essays, *Ancient Slavery and the Ideal of Man*, trans. Thomas Wiedemann (Cambridge, Mass.: Harvard University Press, 1975), 188–210, at 195–96; and Finley, *Ancient Slavery and Modern Ideology*, 91–92, 162, 291 (critical of Vogt's approach).

139. John Selden (1584–1654): English jurist, statesman and archaeologist. The work Capitein refers to was an attempt to describe the law of nature within rabbinical traditions: John Selden, *De jure et gentium juxta disciplinam Hebraeorum* (Wittenberg, 1665) vol. 6.7. On his life and scholarship see John Edwin Sandys, *A History of Classical Scholarship*, vol. 2 (Cambridge: Cambridge University Press, 1908), 322–24.

140. Albert Schultens (1686–1751): Celebrated scholar of Arabic and Hebrew, professor of oriental languages at Leiden from 1732 to 1740. The text referred to here may be his commentary on the book of Job (1737). See SHE vol. 10.276.

141. This passage contains various laws protecting human beings, in this case securing leniency for a slave that has been injured: *When a slaveowner strikes the eye of a male or female slave, destroying it, the owner shall let the slave go, a free person, to compensate for the eye.* This comes immediately after the famous law of retaliation or "lex talionis" (*Eye for eye, tooth for tooth...*): in its own context, this should itself be understood to be a limit on unending revenge.

142. *Now the Lord is the Spirit, and where the Spirit of the Lord is, there is freedom* (II Corinthians 3:17).

For freedom Christ has set us free. Stand firm, therefore, and do not submit again to a yoke of slavery (Galatians 5:1).

Jesus preaches on the Mount of Olives in Jerusalem: *But you will know the truth, and the truth will make you free* (John 8:32). When they ask, in reply, what is meant by "free," Jesus answers, significantly: *Very truly, I tell you, everyone who commits sin is a slave to sin* (8:34).

You were bought at a price; do not become slaves of human masters (I Corinthians 7:23). The argument in this section of the letter is that, since the end of the world is near at hand, it is better for everyone to retain his or her current situation rather than to try to improve it in this life (7:14–24).

143. In Paul's *Letter to the Hebrews* (12:20), the Old Covenant given to Moses is contrasted with the New Covenant embodied in Christ: *For [the Israelites] could not endure the order that was given,"If even an animal touches the mountain, it shall be stoned to death."* In Acts 15:10 Peter asks the disciples: *Why are you putting God to the test by placing on the neck of the disciples a yoke [i.e. of the law] that neither our ancestors nor we have been able to bear?*

144. *Slaves, obey your earthly masters with fear and trembling, in singleness of heart, as you obey Christ.* And *Let all who are under the yoke of slavery regard their masters as worthy of all honor, so that the name of God and the teaching may not be blasphemed.*

145. Franciscus Gregorius Raphelengius, Francis de Ravelinghen (1539–1597): scholar of Hebrew and Persian literature. See BWN vol. 16.72.

146. This is a quotation from Ovid, *Fasti* 1.485–86.

147. In Exodus 32 the Israelites become restive while awaiting the return of Moses, their leader, who had been on Mount Sinai for forty days and forty nights receiving the covenant from God. In its stead, Aaron had the image of a golden calf molded out of their rings, as a symbol of God. The calf, a young bull, symbolized fertility in a number of religions of the ancient Near East.

148. *For sin will have no dominion over you, since you are not under law but under grace.*

149. The contrast between the letter (of Mosaic law) and the spirit (of God's love) is made at II Corinthians 3:6 with the aphorism, *the letter kills, but the spirit gives life.*

150. The passage preceding the one quoted above, and which Capitein is here paraphrasing, runs as follows: *Let each of you remain in the condition in which you were called. Were you a slave when called? Do not be concerned about it. Even if you can gain your freedom, make use of your present condition now more than ever. For whoever was called in the Lord as a slave is a freed person belonging to the Lord, just as whoever was free when called is a slave of Christ.* (20–23) See also n. 38 above.

151. Claudius Salmasius, Claude de Saumaise (1588–1653): French classical scholar, learned also in Hebrew, Arabic, Syriac, Persian, and Coptic, professor at Leiden for his last two decades. The defense he wrote for the reign of King Charles I sparked off a series of rejoinders between himself and John Milton. See Peter van Rooden, *Theology, Biblical Scholarship and Rabbinical Studies in the Seventeenth Century* (Leiden: Brill, 1989), 200–204. Sandys, 285–86.

152. Euripides (ca. 485–ca. 406 B.C.E.): One of the great Greek writers of tragedy, along with Aeschylus and Sophocles. In this instance, a messenger-slave is given his freedom spontaneously, because the news he brings to his noble mistress is so welcome.

153. Aeschines Socraticus (4th century B.C.E.) was a pupil of the famous Athenian philosopher and teacher Socrates. His philosophical dialogues were famed for giving a faithful portrayal of the master. The edition to which Capitein refers is that by Petrus Horreus (dialogue 1, p. 4, near the end).

154. Johannes Casparus Suicerus (1620–1684): Swiss theologian and philologist of Greek, Latin, and Hebrew. Work cited is his *Thesaurus ecclesiasticus* (Amsterdam, 1682). See SHE vol. 11.105.

155. Joachim Kühn (1647–1697): A noted scholar and later professor of Greek literature. The reference here is to his most important work, a substantial commentary on the Greek *Varia historia* of Aelian (ca. 170–235 C.E.), a collection of moralizing anecdotes linked mostly with the animal world. His philosophical allegiance was Stoic and trenchantly anti-Epicurean.

156. Johannes Crocius (1590–1659): Reformed theologian and scholar

of oriental languages at Leyden. See F. C. Clause, Johannes Crocius (Marburg, 1857), and SHE vol. 3.307. The passage from Paul's letter reads: *Let all who are under the yoke of slavery regard their masters as worthy of all honor, so that the name of God and the teaching may not be blasphemed.*

157. Henry More (1614–1687): British philosopher, theologian, and humanist, one of the Cambridge Platonists. Capitein may have known the edition of his *Opera omnia* (London, 1708). See Aaron Lichtenstein, *Henry More: the rational theology of a Cambridge Platonist* (Cambridge, Mass.: Harvard University Press, 1962).

158. *Sanctify them in the truth; your word is truth.*

159. This phrase is drawn from the *Invective against Sallust* (chapter 12), wrongly attributed to Cicero. See J. C. Rolfe's LCL edition of Sallust (1985), 512–13.

160. Hugo Grotius (1583–1645): the most significant political theorist of the 17th-century Netherlands, a jurist by profession but also a statesman and theologian. His writings on natural law made him into a founder of modern international law. Parts of Grotius' work can be interpreted as defending slavery, by implication, as part of the the the law of nations, the *ius gentium*. See Huussen, "The Dutch constitution," 102. The letters, reflecting his contact with eminent contemporaries, many of them Protestant theologians, may be consulted in P. C. Molhuijsen and B. L. Meulenbroek, eds., *Briefwisseling van Hugo Grotius* (6 vols., 1928–67). Grotius was also a classical scholar of great distinction: Sandys, 315–19.

161. Paul Voet (1619–1667): Dutch jurist and church historian, son of Gisbertius Voet of the Voetian-Coccesian debates of the Continuing Reformation (see section IV.1 of the introduction). The work cited is his *Commentarius ad institutiones juris* (1868). See BWN vol. 19.304–5.

162. Christian Thomasius (1655–1728): German Lutheran philosopher and jurist, who advocated some radical interpretations of natural law. His chief work was the *Fundamenta juris naturae* (1705), in which natural rights are affirmed. In his writings he favoured practical piety over adherence to theological systems. See further SHE vol. 11.428–29.

163. John Calvin (1509–1564): French Reformed theologian. His masterwork was his *Institutes*, which came to constitute one of the most important statements of Protestant belief. It was published in its final Latin and French versions in 1559 and 1560. It may be consulted in the translation of John Allen, *Institutes of Christian Religion* (Philadelphia, 1936), vol. 2.3, pages xix and 76–92.

164. Gregory of Nyssa (ca. 330–395 C.E.): Bishop of Nyssa in Cappadocia (the mountainous central region of modern Turkey), and author of theological, mystical, and ascetic works; younger brother of Basil of Caesarea, whose ideas he continues. Gregory was in fact unusual among leaders of the early church for condemning the ownership of slaves, which he associated with sinful pride.

165. Constantine (ca. 285–337 C.E.): Roman emperor who gained power through his military success. Following victory over his rival Maxentius at the Battle of the Milvian Bridge (312), he legislated in favour of Christians with the Edict of Milan (313), thereby ending their persecution by the Roman state. He thus reunited the entire Roman empire and made it more receptive to Christianity.

166. Sozomen (d. 450 C.E.): Jurist of Constantinople, who wrote a history of the church covering the period 324–439, ie. continuing the work of Eusebius. Much of his work is based on that of his contemporary church historian Socrates ("Socrates Scholasticus").

167. Nicephorus Callistus Xanthopoulos: Byzantine historian and man of letters, one of the Byzantine Humanists of the 13th–14th centuries. His 23-volume *Ecclesiasticae historiae* ("church histories") remains a major source of modern information about the early Christian church and particularly of its Christological controversies (theological debates on the nature of Christ).

168. Terence, Publius Terentius Afer (ca. 190–159 B.C.E.). A North African who came to Rome as a slave. Following Greek models he wrote comedies in Latin, seven of which still survive. These have been much admired since medieval times for their elegant style. Note the wordplay in Terence's Latin between *libertus* ("freedman") and *liberaliter* ("freely").

169. Augustine of Hippo, Aurelius Augustinus (354–430 C.E.): Christian bishop in Roman North Africa. One of the major thinkers and writers of the Christian church: among a vast theological output, his *Confessions* and *City of God* had particular impact. Several of his doctrines, such as original sin, gained even greater resonance in Reformation theology.

170. Virgil, Publius Vergilius Maro (70–19 B.C.E.): Roman poet, author of the *Aeneid*, which came to be read as the Roman national epic, under the rule of the emperor Augustus. This poem, together with his pastoral poetry, has been extensively read, studied, and imitated since antiquity, and has been perhaps the most frequently cited Latin work.

171. Peter Gudelinus (1550–1619): Dutch jurist and scholar who wrote on theology and Roman law. The work cited is his *Commentarium de jure novissimo* (1620). See BWN vol. 7.534–36.

172. Johannes Molanus (1553–1585): Dutch theologian and ecclesiastical historian. Work cited is *De canonicis libri tres* (1585). See BWN vol. 12.926–27.

173. Paul Christaneus (1553–1631): Dutch jurist and legal historian. The work referred to is his *Practicarum quaestionum rerumque in supremis Belgarum curiis actarum et observatarum decisiones* (1632). See *Biographie nationale de Belgique* (Brussels: H. Thiry, 1873), 4.111.

174. Ulrich Huber (1636–1707): Dutch jurist who wrote on Grotius, Thomasius, and the Roman *Juris corpus*. The work referred to is his *Institutiones et tituli singulares pandectarum* (1698). See further BWN 19.1374–81.

175. Capitein is here referring to the system of "implicit metropolitan manumission" by which he himself became free on arrival in the Netherlands. See section II.1 of the introduction. His own experience thus underlies his statement of general principle here.

176. Of the regions mentioned, those closest to Holland were to the east, in two parts of the Gelderland province of the Netherlands, namely the inland Zutphen Quarter and the coastal Arnhem Quarter (Veluwe). It will be noted that there is no reference to American slavery in this list of regions, or in fact anywhere else in the treatise.

177. Jean Bodin (1529–1596): French jurist and philosopher, one of the very few humanists to denounce slavery explicitly. His *Six Bookes of the Commonweale* (1576) argue for an ideal of absolute sovereignty that would be harmed by the coexistence of slave and free subjects, and attack Aristotle's notion of natural slavery. See D. B. Davis, *The Problem of Slavery in Western Culture* (1966), 111–14, with references. He is cited by Capitein as attacking the harshness of Portuguese slavery, not for his antislavery stance in general.

178. Augier Ghislain de Busbecq (1522–1592): Flemish diplomat and polymath. His *Turkish letters*, sent from the court of sultan Süleyman I the Magnificent at Constantinople to Ferdinand I, are an important source for contemporary Ottoman history.

179. Potgiesserus, or Joachim Potgiesser, wrote an account of Germanic slaves and freedmen from the time of Caesar to the end of the Middle Ages, originally published in 1703. See futher Finley, *Ancient Slavery and Modern Ideology*, 91, 291. The translation of the last phrase takes some liberty with Capitein's text, which is contradictory as it stands. It is possible that a printer's error crept into the text at this point.

180. In Paul's letter he encourages Philemon, the owner, to take back his runaway slave, Onesimus, *no longer as a slave but more than a slave, a beloved brother—especially to me but how much more to you, both in the flesh and in the Lord.*

181. The Dutch Reformed minister and theologian Henrik Velse (1683–1744) wrote about social issues facing the church, including missionary work in foreign lands. See section IV.1 of the introduction.

Index